Changing How We
TEACH AND LEARN
With HANDHELD
COMPUTERS

This book is dedicated to two women who helped me develop and blossom as a teacher, a researcher, and a technologist. My mother, Julia McCauley, lent me her passions for reading and the thrill for tinkering with computers and technology. My colleague in Jamaica, Marjorie McNab, opened my eyes to the potential of changing how we teach and learn with handheld computers. I will be forever grateful to both.

Changing How We TEACH AND LEARN With HANDHELD COMPUTERS

Carolyn Staudt

Foreword by Alan November

CORWIN PRESS
A Sage Publications Company
Thousand Oaks, California

For information:

Corwin Press
A Sage Publications Company
2455 Teller Road
Thousand Oaks, California 91320
www.corwinpress.com

Sage Publications Ltd
1 Oliver's Yard
55 City Road
London EC1Y 1SP
United Kingdom

Sage Publications India Pvt. Ltd.
B-42, Panchsheel Enclave
Post Box 4109
New Delhi 110 017 India

Printed in the United States of America

Library of Congress Cataloging-in-Publication Data

Staudt, Carolyn.
Changing how we teach and learn with handheld computers / Carolyn Staudt.
    p. cm.
Includes bibliographical references and index.
ISBN 0-7619-3995-4 (cloth) — ISBN 0-7619-3996-2 (pbk.)
    1. Education—Data processing. 2. Pocket computers. I. Title.
LB1028.43.S733 2005
371.33'4—dc22   2004020426

This book is printed on acid-free paper.

04   05   06   07   08   10   9   8   7   6   5   4   3   2   1

Acquisitions editor:	Jean Ward
Production editor:	Sanford Robinson
Copy editor:	A. J. Sobczak
Typesetter:	C&M Digitals (P) Ltd.
Proofreader:	Cheryl Rivard
Indexer:	Karen McKenzie

Contents

Foreword

I have known Carolyn Staudt for 15 years. Our introduction took place in a most unusual way. I was helping a foundation, called Pioneering Partners, that provided funds for innovative teachers to disseminate their work. Carolyn's proposal had been selected as a finalist, but everyone who read it had to ask if it was too good to be true. Carolyn, a math/science teacher, had proposed linking an inner-city school with a rural school through a digital network. Student partners would work together online and produce one lab report or test response as a result of their collaboration. This proposal was part of a larger project that involved the interlocking of 11 geodesic domes that she built with community support. These domes were to simulate an undersea research station (in a former cornfield of Ohio), and her students would live and work inside these domes as if they had been sent to the bottom of the sea in a pressurized diving bell. While housed in the "undersea" domes throughout 7 days, her scientist students would conduct oceanography experiments, manage their own society, and share their data with students around the world. All the while, they would be communicating with the above-ocean world through fiber video links.

I had read more than 100 proposals, and nothing else came close to being this fantastic and imaginative. It all sounded like Jacques Cousteau or *20,000 Leagues Under the Sea* meets high-tech classroom. I jumped on a plane to check out these domes and to meet Carolyn Staudt.

Carolyn's proposal had actually understated the magnificence of what she galvanized her community to build. She even had a used research sub, equipped with robotic arms, shipped from England; it was installed in a steel building attached to the domes. Her students were incredibly focused on carrying out their experiments on Tilapia fish from the Amazon, the raising of hydroponic plants, and the monitoring of physiological responses of all students while inside the domes. Carolyn was given the grant, and teachers flocked from across her region to learn how to immerse students in a multidisciplinary learning environment.

It has taken this long for the technology to catch up with Carolyn's vision of immersing students in the active role of being scientists and global communicators. Now, every teacher does not need a million-dollar set of fiber wired domes. We can now outfit every student with more power in their hand then held in all the computers that were installed 15 years ago in that Ohio cornfield.

Changing How We Teach and Learn With Handheld Computers is a result of a decade's worth of Carolyn's work with teachers, designers, and inventors. This material will help any educator who is considering using or who already uses handhelds, from elementary grades through high school. It will help teachers challenge students to achieve new understandings of patterns of data in math, science, and social studies. It proposes a model in which data become the impetus and support for critical thinking and problem solving. It will allow teachers to help their students feel the power of real data that they generate themselves and share with one another. Her crystal-clear examples are rich in content and aligned to standards.

Get ready to ramp up your adventure level for teaching and learning. The future has arrived, and it can be in your hand.

—*Alan November*

About the Author

 **Carolyn Staudt** is a curriculum designer for technology- and Internet-based projects, including Technology Enhanced Elementary and Middle School Science (TEEMSS 1 & 2), JASON Academy, Modeling Across the Curriculum, Models and Data, Mobile Inquiry Computing, Center for Innovative Learning Technologies (CILT), Science Learning in Context (SliC), Virtual High School, Global Learning and Observations to Benefit the Environment (GLOBE), Kids as Global Scientists (KGS), and NetAdventure at the Concord Consortium. She is especially intrigued with allowing students to collect real-time data with portable sensors and probes attached to desktop and handheld computers. She has designed professional development that includes implementation of technology into the classroom curriculum, teacher and student utilization of existing software, design of tailored activities, and manipulation of software up to, and including, scripting as vice president of KidSolve, Inc. She has 20 years of experience teaching science and math, including physics, chemistry, geoscience, and space science. She holds a master's of education in Curriculum and Instruction in Science from Kent State University. She was a Christa McAuliffe Fellow in 1990 and the Fairlawn, Ohio, Citizen of the Year in 1991.

Handheld Computers as Educational Tools

1

Educational tools over the years have ranged from pieces of chalk and slate to pencil and paper, from fountain pens to ballpoint pens. Similarly, materials changed from primers to full sets of texts. As schools and communities built libraries, students were assigned research topics and referred to bound encyclopedias, books, and magazine articles to gather facts and figures. With the arrival of the ditto machine and later the photocopier, teachers reproduced worksheets to provide drill activities and question sheets for practicing and processing classroom learning. The invention of the overhead projector provided a means for making learning more visual and colorful than the old blackboard and further reinforced the role of the teacher as the expert in the classroom. The tools did little to reconstruct the fundamental notion of teacher as imparter of knowledge. Tools and materials evolved, but the classroom roles remained constant until recently. The late 20th century saw the beginning of a transformation in the teaching and in the learning relationships. Frequently, students whose families invested early in home technology at the beginning of the Internet wave would come to school the day after the teacher introduced a new topic or unit and offer, "I found something on the Internet about what you told us yesterday. Would you like me to bring it in?" Then the student would enthusiastically share with the class and teacher the additional background the student had found on the topic. The teacher or a classmate might then ask the student a question about the material. This was the lightning bolt moment when a new kind of electricity began to recharge classrooms and reconfigure learning relationships.

Once learning started to move across the bridge to technology, including Internet access, more changes were bound to come. Unfortunately, the promise often outstripped reality, for a variety of reasons both technological and human. By the close of the 20th century, adventuresome teachers in well-funded schools were incorporating technology directly into learning as they sent students to computers for information, powerful processing tools and simulations, and new stimuli for the teaching of critical thinking and problem solving. Still, the hardware and infrastructure costs, as well as the logistics of this kind of learning, challenged many schools and teachers. One of the greatest impediments to full use was that unlike workplace and other similar settings, where it was assumed that no one could accomplish work goals without an individual computer, in schools not every desk had a computer on it for ready individual use. In fact, usage was both limited and complicated. The reason for this was largely but not entirely expense.

We are at a new crossroads, thanks to new technology that scales down the equipment in both cost and size without a substantial sacrifice of power. For the cost of 3 classroom computers, it is now possible to purchase 10 to 12 handheld computers. Putting these new portables in the hands of all students has the capacity to change the way we teach and learn. Teachers will guide student learning experiences and, particularly in our standards-based environment, will align learning experiences to meet those standards. What the new technology allows is for students to meet those standards in individualized ways, collect personally meaningful data, and use it to gain understanding of a larger inquiry process that begins to replicate the thinking and learning processes of real work or advanced study. Students and teachers can share data together and create larger data pools from which to build the skills of deep analysis and further inquiry. Students are likely to ask teachers bigger questions, and teachers are as likely to provide some necessary information and then turn those questions back to students with further questions and suggestions for further inquiry or analysis. The new tools can be used in ways that hugely expand what we think of as the learning space. Teachers and students can develop more collaborative ways of teaching and learning than ever before. Handheld computers can place the student at the center of learning; handheld computers offer such promise.

Both hardware and software evolve overnight, and new tools as well as new capacity for the last "new" tools come to the marketplace every day. One of the most promising technologies for education likely will be cell phones, which are already incorporating communication, Internet research, applications, and photographic capacity. For purposes of this book, we will think of handhelds as a combination of technology that offers this future potential. Specific activities and instructions are offered for these handhelds. As equipment changes, these processes will become models that migrate to new equipment.

FIVE BIG REASONS FOR HANDHELDS IN SCHOOLS

When asked recently what are the top five reasons for using handheld computers in schools, my response was immediate: They provide *equitable access to digital technologies* for all children, they are *intuitive* and easy-to-use learning tools, they are the much-needed future *ubiquitous portable* devices, they promote *collaboration* among students and teachers, and they make it possible for meaningful and *seamless interactions* between multiple applications and peripheral devices.

To make changes in how students are taught and how they learn, teachers need to be prepared to use new tools and to change their roles in the classroom (Darling-Hammond, 1997):

> If teachers are to prepare an ever more diverse group of students for much more challenging work—for framing problems; finding, integrating and synthesizing information; creating new solutions; learning on their own; and working cooperatively—they will need substantially more knowledge and radically different skills than most now have and most schools of education now develop. (p. 154)

Teachers in the field will need initial courage to open the path to these new kinds of learning. I hope that this book will offer support for that journey for both classroom teachers and teachers in training.

Because many new technologies are interactive, it is easier to create environments in which students can learn by doing, receive formative feedback, and continually refine their understanding and build new knowledge. Technology can help to create an active environment in which students not only solve problems but also find their own problems (Bransford, Brown, & Cocking, 1999). When used in a context of student inquiry and critical analysis of a vast amount of information simultaneously, handheld technologies offer a promise to provide the computational power and communication channels to empower the individual learner in and outside school.

Equitable Access to Digital Technologies

All students need to have the benefits of the digital technologies. They all must have access to information, computation, and communications tools that will help them in the future workforce. Keep in mind that these educational benefits are what are important and that the access to the technology is only a means to an end. Today, few students, especially the disadvantaged, have adequate exposure to computers to become comfortable with them as a personal tool. Institutional school computers by nature limit familiarity by restricting use. There are too few computers for the numbers of students, computers are located in overcrowded and overbooked computer labs, and computers and servers do not allow access to stored work outside the school. Research shows that giving students a personal learning device can make learning more meaningful to them. Using handheld computers makes it possible for students to take ownership of their work products and learning. With ongoing access to a handheld computer, students become more autonomous and self-directed in their learning (SRI International & Palm, Inc., 2002). According to the National Center for Educational Statistics (NCES), the ratio of students to computers in elementary and secondary schools in the United States is eight students to one computer in cities and five students to one computer in rural settings (NCES, 2000). For those limited classrooms equipped with between 3 and 10 computers, a student still needs to wait in line behind other classmates to use the technology. The technology becomes an intrusion, not a natural extension of the learning environment.

A handheld computer offers automatic storage, an intuitive pen-based graphical interface, and quick and easy communication with other handheld or desktop computers at any location, in or outside school. To provide digital personal tools that will bridge the digital divide, students must have access where and when they need it. The low costs of handheld computers make it more possible for schools to provide equitable access, leaving no child behind.

Intuitiveness

It is easy to forget that student achievement in school depends in part on what happens outside school. Modern technologies can help make connections between students' in-school and out-of-school activities (Bransford et al., 1999). The students of today grew up using GameBoys™ and video games. They easily manipulate small graphically designed screens to complete tasks. They insert game modules and other peripheral devices such as cameras to create their own gaming environments. Although these portable gaming units are toys, they fulfill many educational needs. Similarly, student use of pagers and cell phones outside school make the new handhelds natural tools for them.

When students have shared their dreams about the design of their own personal educational handheld devices, requests have been remarkably similar, as shown by the research funded by the National Science Foundation (*DataGotchi Deep Dive*, 1998). Students want a personal device that is portable and easy to operate. It should feel like a toy, they say, yet provide the ability to input and analyze data from a wide variety of sources. Often students want the tool to be as powerful as a desktop computer, yet compact enough to wear. Finally, students want wireless connection to the Internet and to other devices.

When teachers are asked about their computing needs (*DataGotchi Deep Dive*, 1998), they focus on reliability and performance rather than size or portability. Teachers are often wary of all technology and fear that they will need elaborate skills to operate or troubleshoot problems. The teacher's ideal device would provide applications that build student inquiry-based skills and track student progress seamlessly. Handheld computers in the classroom must provide a means to communicate and collaborate between the student and the teacher. Like students, teachers demand ease of use. Handheld computers, software, and peripherals that meet most of these needs are now available.

Student Needs

- Personal and portable device
- Ability to create, invent, and imagine
- Useful outside the classroom
- Be a tool, yet feel like a toy
- Work that can be private, shared, and/or published
- Promote reflection
- Multiple representations (e.g., graphs, tables, animations)
- Multiple inputs (e.g., touch screen, optional keyboard, voice, camera, sensor)
- Multiple outputs (e.g., Web page, paper, projection)

Teacher Needs

- Total class participation
- Ease of use
- No downtime
- Inquiry-based activities and applications
- Richer meanings of concepts and student models
- Tight coupling to curriculum and standards
- Recording of process and end product
- Evaluation of performance and response
- Reliable data transfer

SOURCE: Adapted from *DataGotchi Deep Dive* (1998) and unpublished data collected by KidSolve™, Inc.

In the past, successful integration of technology was related to the user's comfort with the technology and its features and functions. Unlike desktop computers, the handheld computer has a remarkably short learning curve, especially for students. Because of their familiarity with gaming devices, students intuitively adopt the handheld as a personal computing device. They quickly find the stylus, tap into applications, and learn methods to enter and "beam" data between devices. Training sessions are no longer days or weeks, but can be measured in minutes. Teachers, on the other hand, take a little longer to learn the functions and are often tentative with the smaller device, but they also learn easily to work with handhelds. The reality is that the technology and technological savvy of this generation of students is different from that for adults. Handheld devices are part of their world already!

Ubiquitous Portability

Students' casual and disjointed use of digital technology in education often impedes learning. They spend valuable time adjusting to different computers and applications, rather than experiencing the technology as a seamless extension of their learning environment. As students are shifted from one institutional computer to another throughout the school, they must familiarize themselves with differences between devices and applications. If the classroom is equipped with a few desktops or laptops, they must walk down the hall to a desktop computer located in a separate computer lab or wait in line. With handheld computers, students could simply reach into their backpacks or pockets whenever they need the digital tool. Future students might even *wear* such small computers!

Students' interaction with computers in a discrete lab environment, dissociated from other learning activities, is not a realistic demonstration of their future digital workplace, where computer use is encountered nearly everywhere, in jobs at every level. Portable handheld computers can be used at any location: in the school hallway, on the school bus, in the field, and at home. Through the attachment of sensors (e.g., light, pH, temperature), cameras, or GPS (global positioning system) units to portable handheld computers, the learning experiences become enhanced and more realistic to the students in and outside the classroom.

Collaboration

Handheld computers have the capability to transmit data from device to device, either by infrared beaming or—with newer models—through radio waves. This means that data, writing, concept maps, graphs, and drawings can be exchanged digitally among the devices without wires. Infrared beaming is limited to relatively short, line-of-sight distances between one handheld computer and another, but it offers a powerful way to share information between team members. Radio transmittance enables a network that can send or receive information from multiple handheld computers, at distances of up to 30 feet. The transfer of data does not need to be restricted to other handheld computers. Other wireless devices, such as GPS units, printers, and sensors, can also transfer data to and from handheld computers.

In addition to supplementing sharing of group information among team members, infrared and wireless beaming affords the opportunity for a joint "collaborative white board" in the classroom. With classroom networks, teachers can require students to send their ideas, solutions, or questions during the instruction, and teachers can make immediate adjustments to account for students' needs and their developing ideas in a learner-centered environment. Students can reveal important contrasts and patterns in mathematical and scientific ideas and connect the learning of each individual with the learning of the group. Teachers can provide each student with frequent, formative feedback, and the teacher receives rapid insight into the current level of understanding throughout the classroom (Roschelle, Penuel, & Abrahamson, 2003). By making it possible for students to share thoughts, predictions, and drawings, teachers can obtain immediate conceptual models from their students. By encouraging students to justify their input on a shared document, teachers can instantly poll students' understanding and adjust lessons accordingly.

Transferred information is digital information, which means that the data are searchable and can be sorted. Students can review group predictions, collaborative sketches, and laboratory results to produce a joint report of their findings. With the use of wireless networking, students also can publish their conclusions on the Web directly from their handheld computers.

Seamless Interactions

But why use a technological device in the classroom that costs more than less-expensive educational tools such as paper and pencils? The answer is quite simple: Relatively low-cost handheld computers can provide additional benefits not found with paper and pencil. How they are used in schools is the determining factor when considering purchasing these devices. If the handheld computer is used to "automate" existing practices, the additional cost is not warranted. "Automating essentially means 'bolting' technology on top of current processes and procedures" (November, 2001, p. xix). If used properly, technology tools can change the focus of the classroom from teacher to student; the flow of information (from data, drawings, sensors, and pictures) also changes. Using handheld computers as an "informating" tool rather than as an automating one empowers students to solve problems. Properly designed and applied technologies can generate information as a consequence of their use. Scientific visualization provides models of how, in the course of the data collection, students can generate new views of that data and therefore support new insights. Digital applications can present teachers with new information about student understanding as students use the technologies.

In the business world, handhelds are often used as organizers and planners, but educational software is steadily increasing the capabilities of the handheld computers to help students engage in inquiry learning and problem solving. Many of the new educational applications written for handheld computers make the exchange of data between several applications possible.

For instance, spreadsheets have been designed to accept data from sensor software. Dictionaries enable words to be transferred into writing programs. Statistical analysis software can operate on imported data from calculators and probe-based data acquisition applications. Annotated notes can be attached to digital picture albums for community or field studies. As additional memory and card slots become available, students will be able to access a vast amount of data anytime, anywhere.

EFFECTIVE USE

Not so long ago, schools prided themselves on the presence of institutional computers, often found in computer labs. Teachers booked computer labs months in advance, and these labs were not accessible to students on demand. In some places, this mode still exists. Where it does, students have had limited access to their own work, based on the scheduling of the computer lab and the limits of the class period. Students have no hope of completing their unfinished work or retrieving their data outside school hours. With the move toward equipping classrooms with one to five desktops, the situation improved somewhat but posed its own problems associated with running two simultaneous learning paths in the classroom because universal access was not possible. Now, however, with a handheld device as a replacement for such institutional devices, all students can have computing power in their hands anytime, anywhere, and for considerably less expense than the desktop computer. On average, an adequate handheld computer with at least 8 MB of memory costs about one fifth the price of a desktop computer found in a typical computer lab, or even less. Keep in mind that this type of handheld computer is more powerful than the old Apple IIe™ and has a faster processor.

The Apple IIe™ had 64K of memory and a 1 MHz processor. A Palm™ Tungsten™ T2 has 32 MB of memory and a 200 MHz processor. The Tungsten™ T2 has approximately 128 times as much memory and 200 times the speed. This generation of Palm™ is approximately equivalent to a PowerMac 7200™. The original Palms were similar to a 1 MB Mac Classic™ (S. Bannasch, personal communication, 2003).

Designers of handheld computers originally viewed them as complements to desktop computers, not as a substitute for them. As a result, rich educational applications such as databases, spreadsheets, survey makers, word processors, and graphing applications must be designed specifically for use on the handheld device. Storage and exchange of data must be easy and reliable for large numbers of students. Although some present applications meet these needs, as demonstrated throughout this book, further development must occur in both the handheld hardware and the accompanying software.

Successful integration challenges teachers and students to use the technology in creative and meaningful ways. Portable handheld computers are well suited for implementing active learning activities that engage students and encourage exploration and collaboration. It is imperative to think of these devices not as a solution but rather as an educational tool that plays a vital role in helping teachers alter and update the teaching style and conception of the classroom to more effectively engage students in complex meaningful learning and prepare them equitably for the demands of higher education and the world of work.

OVERVIEW OF THE BOOK

This book is intended to help elementary, middle, and secondary educators to incorporate the new handhelds into classroom teaching and student learning. It is written to help teachers, school leaders, curriculum designers, technology leaders, and teacher educators in the following ways:

1. By providing teachers with concrete step-by-step examples for how to use handheld technology in their classrooms in ways that will foster critical thinking and more collaborative student-directed learning while meeting standards for content areas and technology integration.

2. By providing principals with a vision and a rationale for the use of more economical and equitable handheld computing devices in order to take teaching and learning to more engaged, collaborative, connected, and powerful levels of student learning.

3. By providing technology planners and leaders, curriculum and instruction leaders, and teacher leaders with sample lessons that they can use with teachers to scaffold their movement toward confident adoption of technology to make learning more meaningful and content more connected to real life, while aligning with content standards and technology integration requirements.

In states and districts where handhelds have been purchased for all students, this book is offered as a launching point for their meaningful incorporation. For teachers and schools that are experimenting, this book is intended as a means to create meaningful models for other educators.

Individual chapters of this book provide teachers with examples of significant and powerful tested learning activities that use handheld computers in and outside the classroom. Each activity comes with student instructions that allow the teacher to try the activity first. Some teachers may want to enlist one of their tech-savvy students as a consultant to test-run the activity and teach it to the teacher before the activity is introduced to the class.

Chapter 2 provides organizational and planning activities that help reveal what students are doing, thinking, and understanding.

Chapter 3 illustrates the integration of easily accessible reference materials linked to motivating and engaging applications for review and exploration of information.

Chapter 4 describes uses of the handheld computer that place students at the center of their own data gathering.

Chapter 5 presents meaningful ways to manipulate and display data to assist in thorough conceptual understanding.

Chapter 6 illustrates how students can communicate easily using a handheld computer to share ideas and collaborate on a joint project.

Chapter 7 promotes personal student evaluation, making it possible for students to support and assess their own individual learning.

Chapter 8 reviews answers to commonly asked questions about handheld computer integration that empower both teachers and students.

Each showcased activity is demonstrated with a specific application on the PalmOne™ handheld computer platform. Many applications are freeware or relatively inexpensive applications. Application suggestions for both the PalmOne™ and Pocket PC platforms are provided when available. Each activity has a suggested grade level and subject, learning outcomes and standards, possible classroom approach, and extensions for other subject areas. Each activity concludes with student processing questions, which can be used to assess student learning.

GOING FORWARD

The new handhelds have capacities beyond even individual desk-based computers; they allow students to beam shared data to one another and continue to learn on the bus and at home. They are ideal tools for integrating problem-based learning that clusters standards across content. Used well, they support evidence-based teaching strategies, including cooperative learning and graphic organizers.

Picture again a student of 150 years ago, touching chalk to a slate. With the same stroke, a student today can graphically reorganize pages of data or open a world of information. In this sea of possibility, teachers become more important than ever as they guide students to be effective, selective, and analytical and as they help students use the new tools with purpose, toward the construction of meaning, understanding, and new knowledge.

Organizing and Planning

2

The original purpose of handheld computers was for them to be an organizational and planning device for the everyday businessperson. Relegated to an electronic date book and contact collector, the original handheld computer had little to offer as a dynamic, interactive educational tool. Original business-related applications did not emphasize the display of material for inquiry, data collection, and student conceptual understanding. After several years of development, however, outstanding software has focused on these educational needs. One of the original attempts to develop handheld computer educational software occurred through the efforts of the Center for Innovative Learning Technologies (www.cilt.org/themes/ubiquitous.html), which in 1999 sponsored a competition for assessment tools, collaboration tools, edutainment/ games, science and mathematics applications, sensor or control, and "age 8 and under" applications on handheld computers. This was the beginning of the development of software that broke the barrier between business and education. After several years of use in the classroom, many activities and applications are in use. The three activities discussed in this chapter are just a small sample of meaningful implementations for organizing and planning activities for the classroom. The activities are designed for your students; you should try them yourself first to be comfortable with each aspect of the technology, as well as to consider questions and challenges you might pose during the activities.

1. DAILY LOG

Overview and Learning Outcomes

Students will create a log of their own daily activities on a spreadsheet and display a pie chart of the percentage of time logged for each activity by creating and using graphing techniques and representations to organize, record, and communicate data. Students will further create inferences from the data displays and apply mathematics in context.

Grade Levels

This activity is appropriate for grade levels 3–8.

Standards

National Council of Teachers of Mathematics

The following standards are from the National Council of Teachers of Mathematics (2000) and can be found online at www.standards.nctm.org/document/chapter1/index.htm

- Numbers and Operations: Understand numbers, ways of representing numbers, relationships among numbers, and number systems
- Data Analysis and Probability: Formulate questions that can be addressed with data and collect, organize, and display relevant data to answer them
- Connections: Recognize and apply mathematics in contexts outside of mathematics

International Society for Technology in Education

The following standards are from the International Society for Technology in Education (2000) and can be found online at http://cnets.iste.org/students/s_stands.html

- Basic operations and concepts: Students are proficient in the use of technology
- Technology research tools: Students use technology tools to process data and report results
- Technology problem-solving and decision-making tools: Students employ technology in the development of strategies for solving problems in the real world

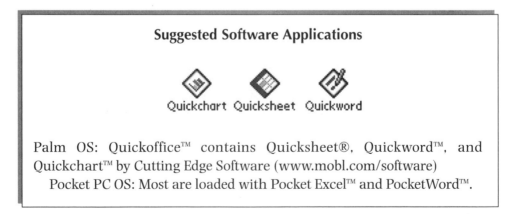

Suggested Software Applications

Quickchart Quicksheet Quickword

Palm OS: Quickoffice™ contains Quicksheet®, Quickword™, and Quickchart™ by Cutting Edge Software (www.mobl.com/software)
Pocket PC OS: Most are loaded with Pocket Excel™ and PocketWord™.

Setting Up Your Spreadsheet

Select Quicksheet® from the Launcher or Home.

Open a new spreadsheet by tapping on Quicksheet at the top of the screen and selecting New.

Name your new workbook Daily Log and tap on OK.

Enter "Activity" into cell A1 and tap anywhere outside the cell.

Enter "Hours" into cell B1 and tap anywhere outside the cell.

Daily Log		▼ Sheet1 ◀▶
	A	B	C
1	Activity	Hours	
2			

List in Column A all the types of activities that you encounter throughout the day. After your last activity, type in the word SUM.

Daily Log		▼ Sheet1 ◀▶
	A	B	C
1	Activity	Hours	
2	sleep		
3	eat		
4	school		
5	computer		
6	bath/brush		
7	tv		
8	play		
9			

Keeping in mind that a day has only 24 hours, it will be extremely helpful to display the sum of your hours as you add them to your spreadsheet for each activity. Tap on the cell next to the SUM and tap on the function icon (fx) on the screen. Scroll through the list and select SUM.

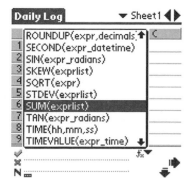

Immediately after selecting SUM, an expression will appear on the function line. Express the list of cells that you wish to be added by tapping and dragging your stylus over the cells in Column B that will fill in the numbers of hours. Once you tap on the green checkmark, a zero should appear in the cell that will display your SUM.

Daily Log		▼ Sheet1 ◀▶
	A	B	C
1	Activity	Hours	
2	sleep		
3	eat		
4	school		
5	computer		
6	bath/brush		
7	tv		
8	play		
9	SUM	0	

✔ =SUM(B2:B8) f_x ▼

Enter the number of hours that you spend on each activity in Column B. If an activity takes a portion of an hour, use a decimal to show the amount. Notice that the number of hours is added as a running total as each new time period is entered. If you exceed the number of hours in a day or want to edit estimates for time spent on an existing activity, you can change any hour value by tapping again on the same cell and typing a new value.

Daily Log		▼ Sheet1 ◀▶
	A	B	C
1	Activity	Hours	
2	sleep	8	
3	eat	1.5	
4	school	7	
5	computer	2	
6	bath/brush	0.5	
7	tv	2	
8	play	3	
9	SUM	24	

Graphing Your Data

Besides reviewing times in your spreadsheet, it is often easier to relate the data by viewing it in graphical form. Tap on cell C1 and again select the function icon (fx). Scroll through the list and select CHART.

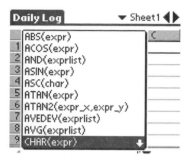

After selecting CHART, an expression will appear on the function line. Tap and drag over the entire range of activities and the number of hours (including the headers). Once you tap on the green checkmark, the word CHART should appear in the C1 cell.

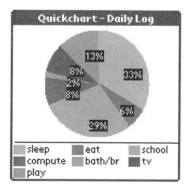

To view your graph, double tap on the word CHART. Select Pie chart by tapping on the pull-down menu. Select Row series. Keep Row and Column labels and show legend with values. Tap on OK.

Try answering the following by reviewing your pie chart.

- How diversified are you in your activities? Design a plan to better distribute your time between family, study, sports, and other areas. (Save your spreadsheet and chart and click on the Launcher or Home and open Quickword™ or Pocket Word to describe your plan.)
- How does your chart compare to those of others in your class? Notice common activities, like sleeping or studying. (Try beaming your chart to other students.)
- Follow your plan and log your activities for 2 weeks. How did your schedule change over time? (Make a spreadsheet that includes the first and last day of each week in subsequent columns on the spreadsheet. Display the results in a bar chart.)

2. AROUND THE WORLD IN EIGHT DAYS

Overview and Learning Outcomes

Students plan round-the-world trips using an integrated mapping program, which enables them to note and record time changes and currency exchange rates between each of their destinations. After students select four of their favorite cities in foreign countries, encourage them to study the time zone changes and currency differences during the overall worldwide trip, thus demonstrating their ability to locate and coordinate information while increasing their knowledge of geographical locations of the world.

Grade Levels

This activity is appropriate for grade levels 3–6.

Standards

National Council for the Social Studies

The following standards are from the National Council for the Social Studies (1994) and are available online at www.ncss.org/standards/toc.html/

- Culture: Experiences that provide for the study of culture and cultural diversity
- Time, Continuity, and Change: Experiences that provide for the study of the ways human beings view themselves in and over time
- People, Places, and Environments: Experiences that provide for the study of people, places, and environments

- Production, Distribution, and Consumption: Experiences that provide for the study of how people organize for the production, distribution, and consumption of goods and services

National Council of Teachers of Mathematics

The following standards are from the National Council of Teachers of Mathematics (2000) and can be found online at www.standards.nctm.org/document/chapter1/index.htm

- Number and Operations: Compute fluently and make reasonable estimates

International Society for Technology in Education

The following standards are from the International Society for Technology in Education (2000) and can be found online at http://cnets.iste.org/students/s_stands.html

- Basic operations and concepts: Students are proficient in the use of technology
- Technology research tools: Students use technology tools to process data and report results
- Technology problemsolving and decision-making tools: Students use technology resources for solving problems and making informed decisions
- Technology problem-solving and decision-making tools: Students employ technology in the development of strategies for solving problems in the real world

---

Suggested Software Application

Palm OS and Pocket PC OS: WorldMate by MobiMate (www.mobimate.com)

Navigating the World

Select WorldMate from the Launcher or Home.

Select your starting destination in the World Map view from the pull-down menu by tapping on the arrow below the map.

Note that once you have selected your home location, you will be able to see the time of day and whether it is light or dark at your location. If the time is incorrect, tap on World Map and select from Options to set your home time correctly. Tap OK to return to the map.

Now click on the map to investigate possible locations around the world you might want to visit.

Select four locations and tap on the clock at the bottom of your screen. Click on the arrows below the smaller clocks and select your foreign destinations.

Tap on Time Calc and select your home and foreign cities. Review the times and make sure that you are sequentially visiting the cities in your around-the-world trip. If not, rearrange in the appropriate order. How many time zones did you cross?

Exchanging Money

Tap on the suitcase at the bottom of the screen and select Edit Categories from the pull-down menu.

Tap on New and create a Countries category. Tap on OK.

Select Countries from the pull-down menu. Select New. Type the name of your first country. Also, place the name of a small gift you would like to purchase and the cost in U.S. dollars. Tap OK. Repeat this for each location.

```
┌─────────────────────────────────────┐
│ Packing List  ▼ Countries           │
│  ┌──────────────┬──────────────────┐│
│  │   My List    │    Full List     ││
│  ├──────────────┴──────────────────┤│
│  │ ☐ Rome painting - $200          ││
│  ├──────────────────────────────────┤│
│  │       Packing List Details       ││
│  │ Category:  ▼ Countries           ││
│  │ Description:                     ││
│  │ Rome painting - $200-$217 Eur    ││
│  │ ................................ ││
│  │ ☐ Already Packed                 ││
│  │ ( OK ) ( Cancel ) ( Delete... )  ││
│  └──────────────────────────────────┘│
└─────────────────────────────────────┘
```

Tap on the dollar sign at the bottom of the screen. Use the pull-down menus to select each country's currency in order to convert U.S. dollars. Rome, Italy, now uses the European currency (the "euro"), but it is also possible to show the Italian lira. These rates change daily and can be obtained from the Web and modified from the Options menu.

```
┌─────────────────────────────────────┐
│ Currencies                          │
│   ▼ USD      ▼ ITL       ▼ EUR      │
│ ▲ 200        420334      217.084    │
│ ▼                                   │
│                                     │
│                                     │
│  1 ▼ USD = [ 2101.671 ]  ITL        │
│            [ 1.085 ]     EUR        │
│ (Get Updated Rates)(Convert)(Clear) │
│  [🌐][🕐][$][⇄][👤][👕][💼]         │
└─────────────────────────────────────┘
```

Open your suitcase and place the local currency cost next to each gift. Which country has the best exchange rate?

Travel Itinerary

Tap on the suitcase again. Tap on each location and plan the number of days that you will remain in each city.

Try answering the following by reviewing your trip itinerary:

- How realistic is your itinerary? Determine the actual distance between each location and estimate 200 miles/hour for flight time to reach your new location. Have you scheduled enough time for flights between destinations? (Use another handheld computer software application to determine the distance between each of your sites. Palm OS: CityZen www.cs.man.ac.uk/~hancockd/CityZen/or Pocket PC OS: Travel Companion by COSMI www.cosmi.com/html/product%20pages/palm_pocket_pc/travel_companion.htm)
- What other information about each of your foreign cities, other than time zones and currency, can you describe? (Use another handheld computer software application to describe other information about the selected cities. Palm OS: Cima World Traveler www.palmblvd.com/software/pc/Cima-World-Traveler-2002-3-26-palm-pc.html or Pocket PC OS: Travel Companion by COSMI (www.cosmi.com/html/product%20pages/palm_pocket_pc/travel_companion.htm)
- Create a report about your worldwide trip. Create a written or graphical presentation document that includes all information about your trip. Palm OS: Quickword™ or QuickPoint™ by Cutting Edge Software (www.mobl.com/software/) or Pocket PC OS: Pocket Word™ with iPresentation Mobile by Presenter Inc. (http://try.webex.com/mk/get/presenter-hp?TrackID=1001054)

3. DISPLAYING STUDENT MODELS

Overview and Learning Outcomes

A mental model is a description of a phenomenon in terms of things that can't be seen, felt, or heard, but explains what the student thinks is going on.

This private and cognitive representation is difficult to elicit from students. The handheld computer makes it possible for students to build their own meanings by describing processes and testing and predicting results of experimentation in various ways (Staudt & Horwitz, 2001). When students express their models in a public forum for others to interact with, they are challenged to revise their mental models. In this activity, students illustrate their understanding of a concept by designing an animation displaying a working model of a concept. Specifically, students visualize a model of gas molecules in an operating piston to demonstrate their understanding of Boyle's Law.

Suggested Software Applications

Sketchy

Palm OS: Sketchy by HI-CE (www.handheld.hice-dev.org/)
   Pocket PC OS: Sketchy by GoKnow (http://goknow.com/Products/Sketchy) available soon

---

Grade Levels

This activity is appropriate for grade levels 9–12.

Standards

National Academies of Science

The following standards are from the National Academies of Science (1996) and can be found online at www.nap.edu/readingroom/books/nses/html/6d.html#csc58

- Science as Inquiry: Recognize and analyze alternative explanations and models
- Understanding About Scientific Inquiry: Scientific explanations must adhere to criteria, such as that a proposed explanation must be logically consistent; it must abide by the rules of evidence; it must be open to questions and possible modification; and it must be based on historical and current scientific knowledge
- Physical Science: Structure of matter
- Physical Science: Structure and properties of matter
- Physical Science: Interactions of energy and matter

International Society for Technology in Education

The following standards are from the International Society for Technology in Education (2000) and can be found online at http://cnets.iste.org/students/s_stands.html

- Basic operations and concepts: Students are proficient in the use of technology
- Technology productivity tools: Students use productivity tools to collaborate in constructing technology-enhanced models, prepare publications, and produce other creative works
- Technology problemsolving and decision-making tools: Students employ technology in the development of strategies for solving problems in the real world

Setting Up Your Spreadsheet

Select Sketchy from the Launcher or Home.

Open a new sketch by tapping on New at the bottom of the screen.

Name your new sketch for a concept with your name and tap on OK.

Select the Draw tool by tapping on the pencil on the bottom left of the screen. This will open a toolbox with various options, including lines, squares, circles, and stored icons. Select your favorite.

If you wish to select a certain color to draw or fill with, tap on the Color tool (black circle) at the bottom of the screen. When you have selected a color, the Color tool will display that color on the screen.

Because this will eventually be an animated series of drawings showing a moving piston, draw a large box on the screen to represent the container that will hold the piston. This "box" will become the background on each consecutive screen when you select Set As Background from the Frame menu.

Now you are ready to add text or drawings to each page. After one page is completed, tap on the arrow to move forward to the next page.

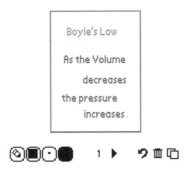

Like the small bouncing atoms, you can copy and paste repeated objects by selecting the Capture tool from the Draw toolbox. Tap and drag across the object that you would like to copy. A black box will appear around the object.

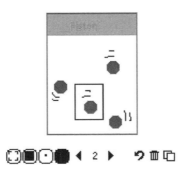

Select Copy Selected from the Edit menu. Place the object in another location on the same page or on a later page by selecting Paste from the same menu.

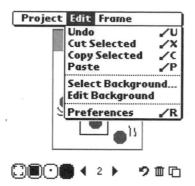

The pasted object will appear in the upper left of the screen inside a black box. Tap on the box to move the object to the desired location.

Continue adding pages to describe how your model functions.

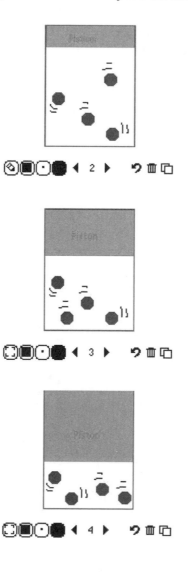

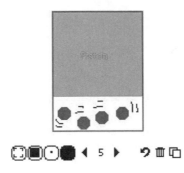

Animating Your Model

To see your animation, select Preferences from the Edit menu. Decide how fast and the direction that you would want your animation to run. Circular will finish and start again from the beginning. Yo-yo will finish and start the animation again from the end.

Select Play animation from the Project menu to watch it run.

Try answering the following by reviewing the animated model:

- How reasonable is the model? Can you describe the model in words? (Use the last page of your animation to describe and justify your model.)

- How does the model compare to those of others in your class? Is there more than one way to model a concept? (Exchange models with another person by using Beam Project from the Project menu. Discuss and adjust the models accordingly.)
- Challenge the model so that a student needs to explain "what if" situations. In the case of the model pictured below, does the student include a model that displays collisions with the container and other molecules? Does the student have an accurate meaning of pressure? When asked, this student replied that pressure represented in the model showed "force per unit area." The student could not explain how the model showed more pressure other than the molecules were closer together and that the amount of pressure displayed by the vibration lines were the same for each frame. After closer analysis, the student revised his model to include collisions of the molecules with both the walls and other molecules, showing a transfer of pressure between the various molecules.

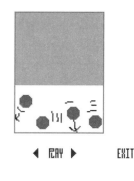

Referencing Information 3

The information age has released a deluge of data that at one time was manageable within textbooks and teachers' heads. During my high school and college studies of chemistry many years ago, students were instructed to memorize the periodic table for exams and tests. It was not until I had taught high school for several years that my students were finally provided with a copy of the periodic table during testing so that they could concentrate on the trends instead of recalling the order of the elements. What a novel idea!

Because reference materials in libraries in the past were related to encyclopedias or nonsearchable static entities, students were tied to card catalogs and the books or magazines that resided on the shelves of the library or classroom. The use of handheld computers introduces the chance to link to other applications seamlessly no matter whether students are in the school or in the field. Copying and pasting information from one application quickly and easily to another offers the chance to utilize the rich bank of knowledge of a reference bank with the use of digital capabilities. The new NWF® Handheld Guide to Birds by eNature.com® at www.enature.com/handheld/handheld_product.asp is a wonderful example of a robust field guide that fits in your pocket. This portable digital field guide permits students to search for birds by name, size, group, and color when they sight a bird; students can listen to a bird sound for easy recognition while in the field.

Selecting reference materials in one application enables a user to merge material accessed for a specific purpose and isolated for review and testing in another setting. The following activities provide an opportunity for students to improve their knowledge of spelling, periodic tables, and star charts by accessing data in an interactive form.

1. SPELLING BEE

Overview and Learning Outcomes

Students build vocabulary lists and design a quiz program to enrich their spelling and vocabulary skills. By using interactive technology tools, students apply knowledge of language conventions; they modify and extend their use of a written language by exercising their writing and communication skills.

Grade Levels

This activity is appropriate for grade levels 3–6.

Standards

National Council of Teachers of English

The following standards are from the National Council of Teachers of English (1998) and are available online at www.readwritethink.org/standards/

- Students apply their knowledge of word meaning and of other texts and their word identification strategies
- Students apply knowledge of language structure and language conventions (e.g., spelling and punctuation)

International Society for Technology in Education

The following standards are from the International Society for Technology in Education (2000) and can be found online at http://cnets.iste.org/students/s_stands.html

- Basic operations and concepts: Students are proficient in the use of technology
- Technology productivity tools: Students use technology tools to enhance learning, increase productivity, and promote creativity
- Technology research tools: Students use technology tools to locate, evaluate, and collect information from a variety of sources

---

Suggested Software Applications

Palm OS: SlovoEd (English-English) at Paragon Software (www.penreader.com/PalmOS/SlovoEd.html)

Beret Study Buddy: Vocabulary by Beret (www.beret.com/vocab.html)
    Pocket PC OS: SlovoEd (English–English) at Paragon Software (www.penreader.com/PocketPC/SlovoEd.html) and Pocket Voc by hrfmobile! (www.hfrmobile.com/download_tools.htm)

Setting Up Your Vocabulary List

Select Vocab from the Launcher or Home. Tap on the screen to start the application.

Tap on All Words. Tap on Default List arrow at the top of the screen and select Add New List. Name your new vocabulary list.

Select SlovoEd (dictionary) from the Launcher or home.

Search for a word that you would like to add to your vocabulary list. Select a word and highlight the definition. Select Copy from the Edit menu by tapping on the header at the top of the screen.

Select Vocab from the Launcher or Home. Tap on the screen to start the application.

Tap on All Words. In your vocabulary list, tap on New to create a word listing. Type your new word in the space at the top of the screen. Tap on the line below Definition and select Paste from the Edit menu by tapping on Word at the top of the screen.

```
┌─────────────────────────────┐
│ Word  ▼ CJ's Verbs      [i] │
│ Word: abdicate              │
│ ........................... │
│                             │
│ Definition:                 │
│ give up, such as power, as of│
│ monarchs and emperors, or duties│
│ and obligations             │
│ ........................... │
│ ........................... │
│ ........................... │
│ ........................... │
│ ( Done )(Cancel)(Delete)(Keyboard)│
└─────────────────────────────┘
```

To save the word to your list, tap on Done.

```
┌─────────────────────────────┐
│ All Words  ▼ CJ's Verbs     │
│ abdicate      give up, such as ...│
│                             │
│                             │
│                             │
│                             │
│                             │
│                             │
│                             │
│                             │
│ Tap on a word for more information│
│ ( Done )( New )(Add New List)  [i]│
└─────────────────────────────┘
```

Search for additional words by either typing in the new words on the top line of the SlovoEd dictionary or by scrolling through the word list by tapping on the up and down arrows. Continue the process between the two applications until you have at least 10 words in your list.

```
┌─────────────────────────────┐
│ All Words  ▼ CJ's Verbs     │
│ abdicate      give up, such as ...│
│ babble        divulge informat...│
│ cackle        emit a loud, unpl...│
│ drone         talk in a monoto...│
│ glean         gather, as of as ...│
│ higgle        wrangle (over a ...│
│ mobolize      cause to move a...│
│ nucleate      form into a nucle...│
│ reanimate     give new life or e...│
│ sublime       vaporize and the...│
│ Tap on a word for more information│
│ ( Done )( New )(Add New List)  [i]│
└─────────────────────────────┘
```

Tap on Done when your list is complete.

Your list can be shared with another device by tapping All Words from the top of the screen and selecting Beam This Word List from the Actions menu.

Practicing With Vocabulary Quizzes

Select Vocab from the Launcher or Home. Tap on the screen to start the application.

Tap on Quiz from the Options screen to examine multiple-choice selections. Select the word that matches the definition clue. Tap Done when you are finished.

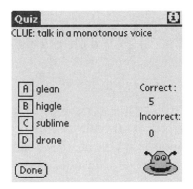

Check out the results of your quiz at any time by tapping on Stats at the bottom of the screen. It is also possible to keep track of the problems that you answered incorrectly by tapping on Answer Track. Tap Done to return to the Options.

To practice spelling your words, tap on Guess? from the Options screen. This is a timed exercise. If you miss a letter, Herbert loses one of his suitcases. Tap Done when finished.

If you are not successful in a specified amount of time or you have selected too many possible letters, the correct answer will appear. Again, you can track your misspellings in Answer Track. Tap Done to return to Options.

Tap on another quiz called Tic Tac Toe on the Options screen. This collaborative quiz makes it possible for you to participate with a partner by receiving an X or O when a correct definition answer is provided for a clue.

Tap on the heads at the bottom of the screen to play with a partner on the same handheld. There is also an option in the middle to play against the handheld and another one on the right to play against another device while beaming. Tap on the square that you would like to occupy if you answer the definition clue correctly. Select the word that best describes the definition clue. Tap on Done to return to the Tic Tac Toe board.

Continue taking turns until someone or the board wins the game. Each player must select a correct answer to mark the spot. Each player's score is shown on the screen. Tap Done to return to Options.

Expanding Your Vocabulary

Create additional vocabulary lists for nouns, adjectives, or synonyms. Practice each list. What is your overall percentage of success? Which words do you most often miss? Practice using these words in sentences.

Write a short story using all the words in one of your lists using a word processing document (Palm OS: Quickword™ by Cutting Edge Software (www.cesinc.com/) or Pocket PC OS: Pocket Word™). Share this document with another student or your class.

2. CHEMICAL PERIODICITY

Overview and Learning Outcomes

Students brainstorm questions about the periodic table and its trends. The iKWL (I know, I wonder, I learned . . .) application makes it possible for students to investigate research materials such as articles, Web sites, or in this case, a chemical periodic table. Students can form their own word lists before observing the periodic table, use these words to construct ideas from the observed trends on the periodic table, and research the concepts in other materials. By using interactive technology tools, students formulate and revise their own questions and findings.

Suggested Software Applications

Palm OS: Ultimate PTE by stand alone, inc. (http://standalone.com/palmos/periodic_table/)

iKWL by Hi-CE (Center for Highly Interactive Computing in Education at the University of Michigan) (http://palm.hice-dev.org/beta.php)

Pocket PC OS: PocketChemistry by RA Software (www.pocketchemistry.com/)

iKWL: Brainstorming by GoKnow (http://goknow.com/index.html), available soon

---

Grade Levels

This activity is appropriate for grade levels 9–12.

Standards

National Academies of Science

The following standards are from the National Academies of Science (1996) and can be found online at www.nap.edu/readingroom/books/nses/html/6d.html#csc58

- Science as Inquiry: Formulate and revise scientific explanations and models using logic and evidence
- Understanding About Scientific Inquiry: Scientific explanations must adhere to criteria, such as that a proposed explanation must be logically consistent; it must abide by the rules of evidence; it must be open to questions and possible modification; and it must be based on historical and current scientific knowledge
- Physical Science: Structure of matter
- Physical Science: Structure and properties of matter
- Physical Science: Chemical reactions

International Society for Technology in Education

The following standards are from the International Society for Technology in Education (2000) and can be found online at http://cnets.iste.org/students/s_stands.html

- Basic operations and concepts: Students are proficient in the use of technology
- Technology productivity tools: Students use productivity tools to collaborate in constructing technology-enhanced models, prepare publications, and produce other creative works
- Technology research tools: Students employ technology to locate, evaluate, and collect information from a variety of sources

Formulating Your Thoughts

Select iKWL from the Launcher or Home. Tap on the screen to start the application.

Open a new project by tapping on New at the bottom of the screen.

Name your new project based on your investigations and tap on OK.

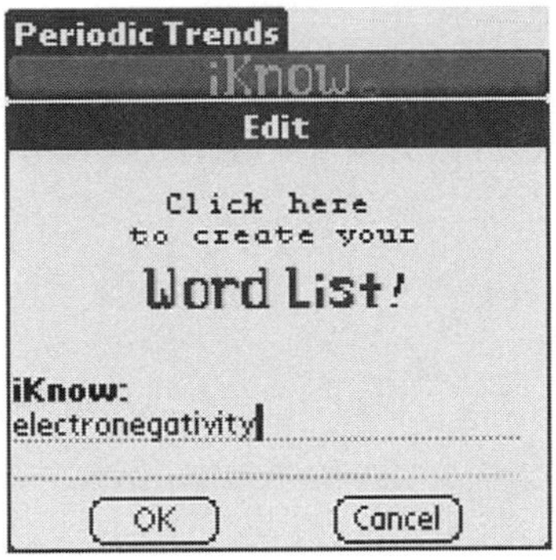

Periodic Trends

iKnow

Edit

```
Click here
to create your
```
Word List!

iKnow:
electronegativity

(OK)   (Cancel)

Tap on iKnow to create your word list of properties that you would like to investigate. Additional properties can be added once you investigate the periodic table.

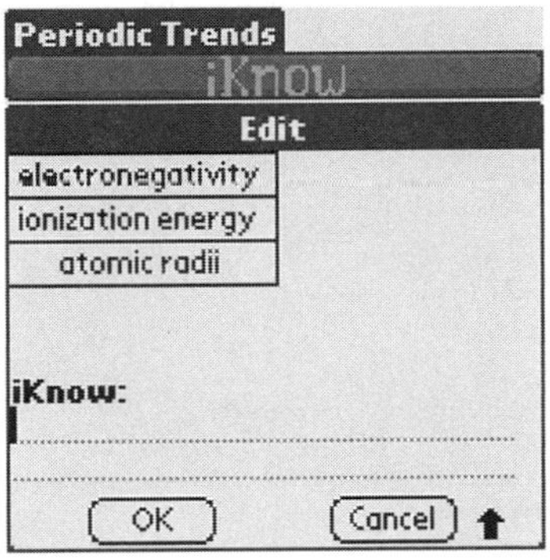

Periodic Trends

iKnow

Edit

electronegativity
ionization energy
atomic radii

iKnow:

(OK)   (Cancel) ↑

After entering the initial words that interest you, tap on each property to elaborate what you know prior to your investigation of the periodic table.

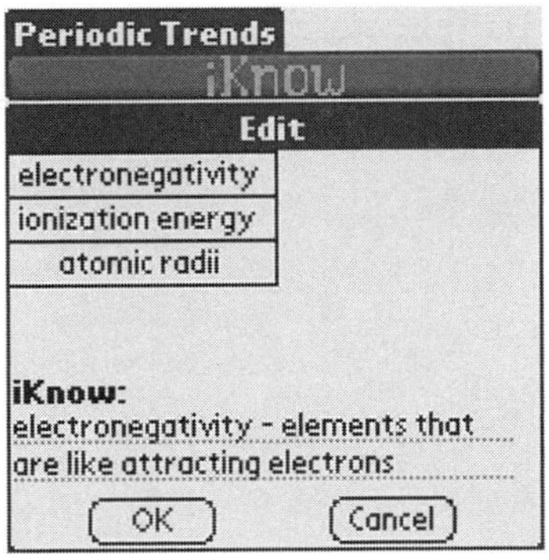

Periodic Trends

iKnow

Edit

electronegativity
ionization energy
atomic radii

iKnow:
electronegativity - elements that
are like attracting electrons

(OK)   (Cancel)

Tap on OK to view your complete list and descriptions. If the length of the descriptions is larger than the available space on the screen, two arrows will appear to the right of the entries. Tap on the arrows to move through the descriptions.

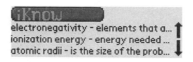

Reviewing Periodic Trends

Select PTE from the Launcher or Home. Tap on the screen to start the application.

Tap on any colored square on the periodic table. Notice that the name, symbol, atomic weight, and atomic number of the selected element are shown at the top of the screen.

Continue to tap around the screen and compare the properties of different elements. Scroll through the properties by using the slide bar on the right of the screen.

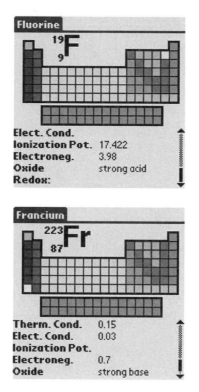

Look for the chemical properties that you listed in iKWL. Do the properties vary widely from one part of the table to another part? For example, the electronegativity of fluorine on the upper right of the table is almost 4, whereas the electronegativity of francium on the bottom left is less than 1. Why is this so?

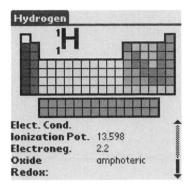

How does the number of electrons in a particular shell or energy level affect the electronegativity? How does the electronegativity of elements change within the same family? Does it increase or decrease? How does this compare to your hypothesis?

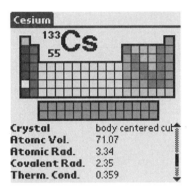

Continue to investigate properties such as atomic radii and ionization energy. How do these properties relate to electronegativity?

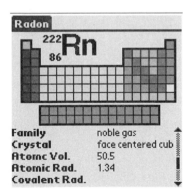

At any time you can reopen iKWL to record your findings in iLearned. Simply tap on iLearned and tap on the word for which you have discovered information.

Periodic Trends
iLearned
Edit
electronegativity
ionization energy
atomic radii

iLearned:
Highly electronegative elements
have few electrons in outside.|
OK   Cancel

Formulating Questions

Once you are finished investigating the periodic table, reopen iKWL and tap on iWonder and express any questions that you still have about the listed chemical properties.

Periodic Trends
iKnow
electronegativity - elements that a...
ionization energy - energy needed ...
atomic radii - is the size of the prob...
iWonder
Why is this occur?
Where does the energy come from?
What is shielding?
iLearned
Highly electronegative elements ha...
Noble gases have high ionization en...
They get larger as you go down gro...

Revisit the periodic table to try to answer some of your questions. Use other resources to search for answers. Revise what you learned and your questions accordingly.

Share and discuss your revised list of questions with your classmates and teacher. Again, revise both what you learned and your question list.

Use any additional resources (e.g., eBooks, textbooks, Internet) to continue to answer and revise what you learned and your questions.

Propose and design an investigation to help you find a solution to any remaining questions (Palm OS: Quickword™ by Cutting Edge Software (www.cesinc.com/) or Pocket PC OS: Pocket Word™). Consult your teacher before performing any activity in the laboratory. Review the results of the investigation and revise what you learned and your questions. Investigations of this kind will often answer some questions but also may introduce additional questions that will spark further work.

3. STARRY SKY

Overview and Learning Outcomes

Students observe objects in the sky while looking at a camera-like display of the stars and planets on the handheld. Students locate constellations, comets, and asteroids at various times and dates from different viewing directions. Students gain an appreciation of our solar system and the dynamic nature of the Earth and the sky after completing daily observation logs.

Grade Levels

This activity is appropriate for grade levels 9–12.

Standards

National Academies of Science

The following standards are from the National Academies of Science (1996) and can be found online at www.nap.edu/readingroom/books/nses/html/6d.html#csc58

- Science as Inquiry: Ask a question about objects, organisms, and events in the environment
- Understanding About Scientific Inquiry: Scientific explanations must adhere to criteria, such as that a proposed explanation must be logically consistent; it must abide by the rules of evidence; it must be open to questions and possible modification; and it must be based on historical and current scientific knowledge
- Earth and Space Science: Objects in the sky
- Earth and Space Science: Changes in earth and sky
- Science and Technology: Abilities to distinguish between natural objects and objects made by humans

International Society for Technology in Education

The following standards are from the International Society for Technology in Education (2000) and can be found online at http://cnets.iste.org/students/s_stands.html

- Basic operations and concepts: Students are proficient in the use of technology
- Technology productivity tools: Students use productivity tools to collaborate in constructing technology-enhanced models, prepare publications, and produce other creative works

• Technology problem-solving and decision-making tools: Students employ technology in the development of strategies for solving problems in the real world

---

Suggested Software Applications

Planetarium

Palm OS: Planetarium by Andreas Hofer Software at (www.aho.ch/pilotplanets/)

Pocket PC OS: The Sky Pocket Edition at SoftwareBisque at (www.bisque.com/Products/TheSkyPE/TheSkyPE.asp)

Calibrating the Star Map for Your Location

Select Planetarium from the Launcher or Home. Tap on the screen to start the application.

Select Set Location from the options menu. Enter the latitude and longitude of your specific location.

If you do not know the latitude and longitude of your exact location, Tap on the Pick button and select the city closest to you. Tap on the scroll bar to view cities in the United States and other countries. Highlight the city of choice and tap on OK.

Locations	▼ America
Bloomington, IL	40.5°N, 89.0°W
Bogota	4.6°N, 74.1°W
Boise, ID	43.6°N, 116.2°W
Boston, MA	**42.3°N, 71.1°W**
Boulder, CO	40.0°N, 105.3°W
Brasilia	15.8°S, 47.9°W
Bridgeport, CT	41.2°N, 73.2°W
Buenos Aires	34.6°S, 58.5°W
Burlington, VT	44.5°N, 73.2°W
Calgary, AB	51.0°N, 114.1°W
Cali	3.5°N, 76.5°W

(OK) (Cancel) (New) (Details...)

Set both the date and time from the Options menu.

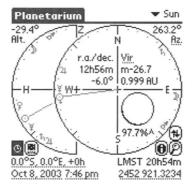

Select the Compass View from the Options menu or by tapping on the Compass icon. Notice the sky objects that should be visible at your location.

Planetarium   ▼ Sun

-29.4° Alt.   263.2° Az.

r.a./dec. Vir
12h56m m-26.7
-6.0° 0.999 AU

97.7%⅄

0.0°S, 0.0°E, +0h   LMST 20h54m
Oct 8, 2003 7:46 pm   2452 921.3234

View a list of the objects and their symbols by tapping on the Rise and Set Table.

Selected Objects   ℹ️

☑ 1 ☉ Sun
☑ 2 ☽ Moon
☑ 3 ☿ Mercury
☑ 4 ♀ Venus
☑ 5 ♂ Mars
☑ 6 ♃ Jupiter
☑ 7 ♄ Saturn
☑ 8 ♅ Uranus
☑ 9 ♆ Neptune
☑ 10 ♇ Pluto
☐ 11 ⚹ Bootes (Herdsman)
☐ 12   <none>

(OK) (Cancel)

Viewing the Sky

Select the Sky View from the Options menu or by tapping on the Sky View icon on the screen.

Tap on any object to show its name and relative location.

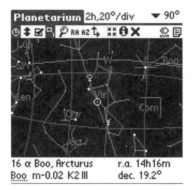

Move the display field by holding down and dragging the stylus.

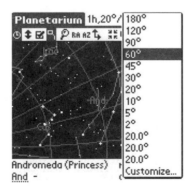

Use the pull-down menu in the upper right corner to zoom in or out.

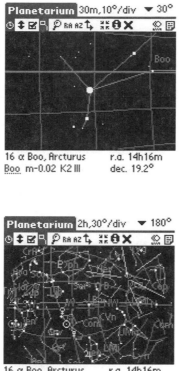

The two dials at the bottom right of the screen allow you to indicate your viewing direction. To set the altitude of the center of the star map, tap on the dial on the left. To set the azimuth, tap on the dial on the right.

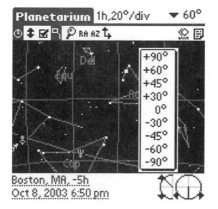

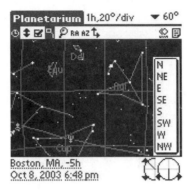

Make the star map visible outside at night by selecting the Night Mode from Preferences on the Options menu. How does the night sky in your area compare to the star map?

Tap on the Full Screen icon to enlarge the sky map. Tap again on the icon to return to normal-size screen with the toolbar visible.

Tap on the Constellation icon to toggle between the stars with and without the constellation lines.

Locating and Learning About Objects in the Sky

Tap on the Search icon to select and highlight a specific sky object. Additional objects are available from the pull-down menu.

Tap on the selected object from the list. The screen will return to the sky map with a red cross marking the selected object.

Tap on the Information icon to observe details about the object.

Tap on all of the options at the bottom of the information page to view positioning and rising/setting times.

Logging Your Observations

Locate the selected object in the night sky. Tap on the Observation icon and tap on the New button. Locate your object by tapping and scrolling through the List.

Record your description and comments in the Observation Log and tap on the Done button when finished. Tap on the Sky View icon to return to the star map.

Try answering the following questions after investigating and logging observations over a 1-week period for four additional deep sky objects.

- How does the brightness of the stars relate to the star's distance from you?
- The star map shifts ever so slightly over time. Is there a reason for this? How does the view direction change on the two dials on the bottom right of the screen with each new star map?

Track and log the shape and location of the Moon over the period of 1 month. Why do portions appear to disappear? Select the Moon from the planet search list. Tap on Stats Information to observe the changing shape of the Moon for the present date. Use the Time button to observe the stats (and shape) for the Moon through the same time period that the logging occurred.

```
┌─────────────────────────────────────┐
│   Object Information            ⓘ    │
│ ☽ Moon                               │
│ Location      Boston, MA, -5h        │
│ Local Time    Oct 15, 2003  8:33p    │
│ Magnitude     -10.9                  │
│ Distance      403e3 km          ◖    │
│ Elongation    117.3°W                │
│ Phase         62.7°                  │
│ Illuminated   72.9%        waning    │
│ Age           19.9326 d   19d22h22m  │
│ Angular Size  29'41"                 │
│                                      │
│   ( OK )  Pos Stats R/S Time Phases  │
└─────────────────────────────────────┘
```

How did your log compare to the stats information? How does the positioning of the Earth and the Sun relate to the change in the shape of the Moon? Explain in detail your understanding of the cause for the difference in appearance of the Moon throughout the month (Palm OS: Quickword™ by Cutting Edge Software (www.cesinc.com/) or Pocket PC OS: Pocket Word™).

Data Gathering $\quad$ 4

Information in the world around us is constantly changing. Common tools that can be used to take snapshots of this timely data include polls, surveys, and databases. Just as the yearly census provides us with a better understanding of a country's population diversity, surveys and polls designed by students make it possible for them to gather data about their surroundings and peers.

In addition, information that students acquire from personal observation leads to curiosity, questioning, reflection, forming interpretations about their environment, and further investigations. This information may be both qualitative and quantitative.

Qualitative observations use the five senses (smell, taste, sight, sound, and touch)—for example, the observation of color, shape, and texture of a leaf (and possibly fragrance and taste, too). Quantitative observations, which measure a quantity, require an additional reference tool, such as a ruler to measure the length of a leaf. Gathering and classifying this data helps to provide order through observing similarities, differences, and interrelationships.

Sensors attached to a handheld computer through a variety of hardware interfaces enable students to gather quantitative data. These technologies give the learner new ways to explore and understand the world beyond the capabilities of their senses. How many substances are really safe to taste? Do students have the time to observe a phenomenon for 24 hours? Are they capable of collecting more than 30 temperature readings per second with a simple thermometer to record changes of body temperature during exercise? Sensors enable students to measure physical aspects of their world, such as temperature, light intensity, dissolved oxygen, relative humidity, barometric pressure, and pH. Furthermore, students can take these measurements anywhere, from lab to field to river. Research has found that the ability to take and display real-time readings using different probes and sensors resulted in greater student engagement and enabled students to concentrate on the science rather than logistics in their investigations (SRI International & Palm, Inc., 2002).

One classic experiment in the general science lab studies the phase change of ice. Students are asked to melt a beaker of ice over a heat source while recording the temperature every 30 seconds. After 45 minutes of painstaking data collection, students can create a graph of the change in temperature over time. In the past, students dedicated so much time to creating the graph that they failed to grasp the significance of the data, namely the flat line that appears around the zero degree position on the graph; the graphing exercise itself became the main focus of the activity. Research comparing traditional paper-and-pencil graphing methods with the instantaneous computer displays on machines equipped with sensors shows that students have a significant increase in retention of graph understanding when they see the graph instantaneously while the data are being collected (Brasell, 1987). Beyond this, the sensor electronic transducers are so small and sensitive that lesser amounts of ice water can be tested simultaneously within the same class. Students can also vary the types of ice solutions by adding different amounts and types of salts to the ice water. As a result, the students collecting the temperature data have time to concentrate on the reasons for the flat line and analysis of the heat transfer while they are still in the lab.

The following activities demonstrate proven data collection techniques relevant to students. Students perform surveys for comparisons between different populations, journal daily exercise practices in a database for long-term fitness planning, and research a local pond.

1. SURVEYING HOMEWORK PRACTICES

Overview and Learning Outcomes

Students design and conduct surveys to help them poll their classmates on relevant and salient topics. Through critical analysis of research methods, statistics, and research designs, students are able to observe differences in human behavior. The survey highlighted in this activity was designed to determine if the amount of homework assigned by teachers was acceptable for the average student population—a topic intrinsically motivating to most students!

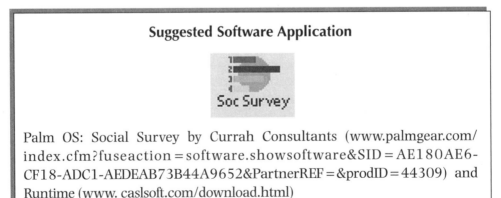

Suggested Software Application

Palm OS: Social Survey by Currah Consultants (www.palmgear.com/index.cfm?fuseaction = software.showsoftware&SID = AE180AE6-CF18-ADC1-AEDEAB73B44A9652&PartnerREF = &prodID = 44309) and Runtime (www. caslsoft.com/download.html)

Pocket PC: Pocket Survey by Pocket PC Survey Software & Systems (www.pocketsurvey.co.uk/)

Grade Levels

This activity is appropriate for grade levels 4–12.

Standards

National Council for the Social Studies

The following standards are from the National Council for the Social Studies (1994) and are available online at www.ncss.org/standards/toc.html/

- People, Places, and Environments: Experiences that provide for the study of people, places, and environments
- Individual Development and Identity: Experiences that provide for the study of individual development and identity
- Individuals, Groups, and Institutions: Experiences that provide for the study of interactions among individuals, groups, and institutions
- Production, Distribution, and Consumption: Experiences that provide for the study of how people organize for the production, distribution, and consumption of goods and services

National Council of Teachers of English

The following standards are from the National Council of Teachers of English (1998) and are available online at www.readwritethink.org/standards/

- Students employ a wide range of strategies as they write and use different writing process elements appropriately to communicate with different audiences for a variety of purposes
- Students conduct research on issues and interests by generating ideas and questions, and by posing problems. They gather, evaluate, and synthesize data from a variety of sources (e.g., print and nonprint texts, artifacts, people) to communicate their discoveries in ways that suit their purpose and audience
- Students use spoken, written, and visual language to accomplish their own purposes (e.g., for learning, enjoyment, persuasion, and the exchange of information)

National Council of Teachers of Mathematics

The following standards are from the National Council of Teachers of Mathematics (2000) and can be found online at www.standards.nctm.org/document/chapter1/index.htm

- Numbers and Operations: Compute fluently and make reasonable estimates

- Data Analysis and Probability: Formulate questions that can be addressed with data and collect, organize, and display relevant data to answer them
- Connections: Recognize and apply mathematics in contexts outside of mathematics

International Society for Technology in Education

The following standards are from the International Society for Technology in Education (2000) and can be found online at http://cnets.iste.org/students/s_stands.html

- Basic operations and concepts: Students are proficient in the use of technology
- Technology research tools: Students use technology tools to process data and report results
- Technology problem-solving and decision-making tools: Students use technology resources for solving problems and making informed decisions
- Technology problem-solving and decision-making tools: Students employ technology in the development of strategies for solving problems in the real world

Creating Your Survey

Select SocSurvey from the Launcher or Home. Run Time software must be loaded before Social Survey is loaded, so it may take several seconds to open.

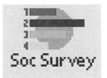

Tap on Files from the Main menu.

Tap on the New button and name your survey. Tap on the Open button and select Setup.

Type in all of your questions. Review the questions and select the type of answer. If you want a checklist, select Edit Coded Answers.

If you want a Yes or No answer, select Y/N from the list. Tap on the Done button when you are finished.

To add other selections, type the choices one at a time on the line and tap the Add button. Tap on Done when you are finished providing all the options for each question.

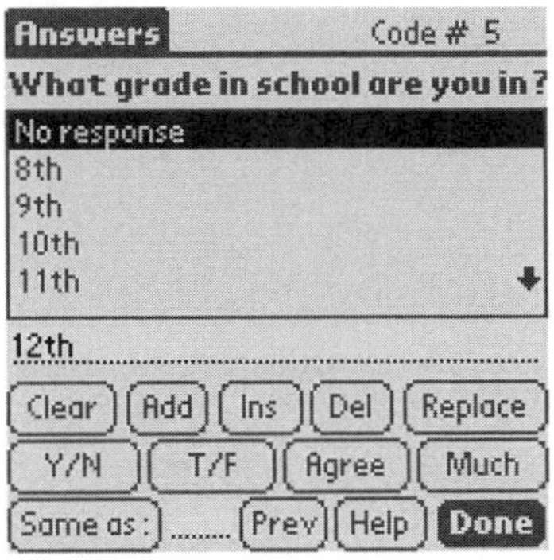

Answers	Code # 5
What grade in school are you in?	
No response	
8th	
9th	
10th	
11th	
12th	
Clear	Add	Ins	Del	Replace
Y/N	T/F	Agree	Much
Same as :	Prev	Help	**Done**

Tap on the Menu button to start using the survey.

Social Survey

Files	Edit Data
Survey	Import
Statistics	Export
Graph	
Help	About

Taking the Survey

Select a participant and have the student tap on the Survey button. Serial numbers are provided for each participant so that responses can be anonymous. The default, if no answer is given, is set for –99. Direct the student participant to tap on the Continue button to start the survey.

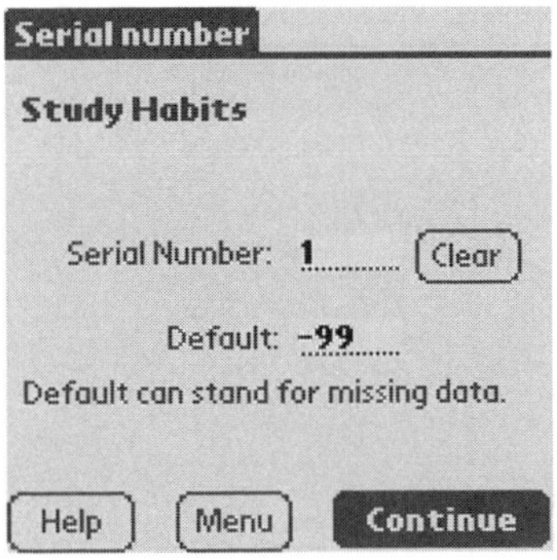

Serial number

Study Habits

Serial Number: **1**....... [Clear]

Default: **–99**.......
Default can stand for missing data.

[Help]   [Menu]   **Continue**

Instruct the participant to tap on the box that best represents the answer for each question.

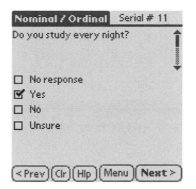

After the participant completes the survey, Save the data. Tap on the Continue button to add another participant or the Menu button to return to the Main menu.

Analyzing the Data

Tap on Statistics to see the options for displaying the variety among the answers provided by the participants.

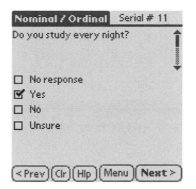

To view the size of the sample and see how the answers varied, select the Descriptive choice. Choose each question by placing the number of the question on the line at the bottom of the screen between the arrows. Tap on the Calc button to observe the size of the sample, median, mean, mode, variance, standard deviation, minimum, and maximum. Tap on the Menu button again to return to the Statistics screen.

```
┌─────────────────────────────────┐
│ Study Habits                    │
│ Do you study every night?       │
│        Size =  10               │
│      Median =  1.50             │
│        Mean =  1.10             │
│        Mode =  1                │
│    Variance =  0.10             │
│    St. Dev. =  0.11             │
│        Min. =  1.00             │
│        Max. =  2.00             │
│ (Menu)     (<) 1.... (>)   Calc │
└─────────────────────────────────┘
```

Tap on the Frequency button. Use the arrows to select the question that you want to review. Tap on the Go button to observe the number of times each answer was selected as well as the response percentage that number represents. Tap on the Menu button again to return to the Statistics screen.

```
┌─────────────────────────────────┐
│ F & %  Var:5  (<)(>) Go (Bar)(Mnu)│
│ n=10 Do you feel that you have too m│
│ 0 0 0.0% (0.0-0.0) (0.0-0.0%)   │
│ 1 6 60.0% (5.7-6.3) (57.0-63.0%)│
│ 2 4 40.0% (3.7-4.3) (37.0-43.0%)│
│ 3 0 0.0% (0.0-0.0) (0.0-0.0%)   │
│                                 │
│                                 │
│                                 │
│                                 │
└─────────────────────────────────┘
```

Tap on the Correlation button. Is there a relationship between the answers for one question and those for another? Type the number of each question on the line on the upper left of the screen to obtain a correlation coefficient between two related variables. The wording for each question will appear next to the line. Tap on the Menu button again to return to the Statistics screen.

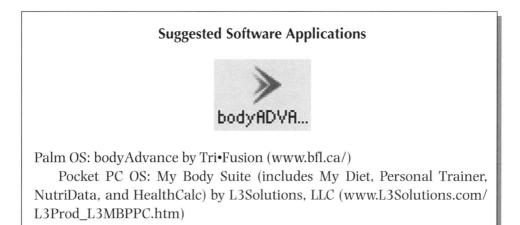

2. FITNESS FOR LIFE

Overview and Learning Outcomes

Students design a long-term fitness plan that maintains a healthy level of fitness and promotes a physically active lifestyle, setting their own personal fitness goals. Students log their daily completion of their plan's exercise routines and their eating and sleeping habits. Through logging their health- and fitness-related behaviors, they become more aware of how their lives are affected by fitness practices.

Suggested Software Applications

Palm OS: bodyAdvance by Tri•Fusion (www.bfl.ca/)
    Pocket PC OS: My Body Suite (includes My Diet, Personal Trainer, NutriData, and HealthCalc) by L3Solutions, LLC (www.L3Solutions.com/L3Prod_L3MBPPC.htm)

Grade Levels

This activity is appropriate for grade levels 5–12.

Standards

National Health Education Standards

The following standards are from Summerfield (1995) and can be found online at www.ericfacility.net/ericdigests/ed387483.html

- Students will comprehend concepts related to health promotion and disease prevention
- Students will demonstrate the ability to practice health-enhancing behaviors and reduce health risks
- Students will demonstrate the ability to use goal-setting and decision-making skills to enhance health

National Academies of Science

The following standard is from the National Academies of Science (1996) and can be found online at www.nap.edu/readingroom/books/nses/html/6d.html#csc58

- Science in Personal and Social Perspectives: Personal health

International Society for Technology in Education

The following standards are from the International Society for Technology in Education (2000) and can be found online at http://cnets.iste.org/students/s_stands.html

- Basic operations and concepts: Students are proficient in the use of technology
- Technology productivity tools: Students use technology tools to enhance learning, increase productivity, and promote creativity
- Technology research tools: Students use technology tools to process data and report results
- Technology problem-solving and decision-making tools: Students employ technology in the development of strategies for solving problems in the real world

Setting Up Your Fitness Journal

Select BodyADVANCE from the Launcher or Home.

Open Goals from the Main menu.

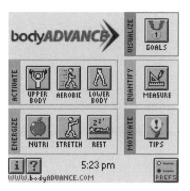

Replace the existing overview with at least five goals. Tap on Home at the bottom left of the screen to return to the Main menu.

Edit Goals

My Goals are:

1. Run at least 1 mile a day and eventually increase to 2 miles.
2. Lose 5 pounds in 2 weeks and maintain this weight loss.
3. Eat three balanced meals a day.
4. Sleep at least 7 hours a day.
5. Lose an inch or two around my waist.

WWW.bodyADVANCE.COM

When initially starting this program, you are prompted to state a start date, which will make it possible for you to enter data in the other menus. Start with the Measure menu by tapping on it. You will need a cloth tape measure or a piece of string, a ruler, and a scale. Select the date to record the measurements. Each week, you should record your weight and circumference measurements.

Measurements

Day:	Date:	Weight:	Waist:
01	5/26/03	130	24
08	6/2/03	0	0
15	6/9/03	0	0
22	6/16/03	0	0
29	6/23/03	0	0
36	6/30/03	0	0
43	7/7/03	0	0
50	7/14/03	0	0

Show: ▼ incomplete

WWW.bodyADVANCE.COM

```
┌─────────────────────────────────────┐
│ Circumference Measurements          │
│ Day:      01   Date:  5/26/03       │
│                                     │
│ Height:    5.5   Waist:      24     │
│ Neck:       13   Hips:       36     │
│ Arms:       10   Thigh:      17     │
│ Chest:      36   Calf:       10     │
│                                     │
│          Status: ▼ incomplete       │
│ Notes:                              │
│ Interesting that I have an extra 12 │
│ pounds of fat.                      │
│ [i][⌂][◄][◄][►][►►]    [▦][♀]       │
│ www.bodyADVANCE.COM                 │
└─────────────────────────────────────┘
```

If you wish to add a motivation for a day, tap on Tips and edit the message.

```
┌─────────────────────────────────────┐
│ Random Tip of the Day               │
│  Tip: 1                             │
│                                     │
│ This is tough, but I can do it. If I am │
│ persistent it will change the way I live. │
│                                     │
│                                     │
│                                     │
│                                     │
│                                     │
│                                     │
│ [i][⌂][◄][◄][►][►►]   ( Edit Tips ) │
│ www.bodyADVANCE.COM                 │
└─────────────────────────────────────┘
```

Recording Your Exercise

Tap on Upper Body, Aerobic, and Lower Body to record your exercise regimen. Select the date and record the regimen. Note that each recorded type is on a different day.

UPPER BODY		AEROBIC		LOWER BODY	
DAY	DATE	DAY	DATE	DAY	DATE
01	5/26/0	02	5/27/0	03	5/28/0
05	5/30/0	04	5/29/0	08	6/2/03
10	6/4/03	06	5/31/0	12	6/6/03
15	6/9/03	09	6/3/03	17	6/11/0
19	6/13/0	11	6/5/03	22	6/16/0
24	6/18/0	13	6/7/03	26	6/20/0
29	6/23/0	16	6/10/0	31	6/25/0
33	6/27/0	18	6/12/0	36	6/30/0

[i][⌂] (Show:) ▼ incomplete
www.bodyADVANCE.COM

Record each exercise based on type and intensity.

Chest			Start:	5:30 am

Day: 01 Date: 7/4/03 Fin: 6:16 pm

1-5: ▼ barbell flat press

6: ▼ dumbbell incline press

S	Weight		Repetitions	Intensity		Rst	Done
1	5	12	12	5	5	1	☑
2	5	10	10	6	6	1	☑
3	0	8	8	7	7	1	☐
4	0	6	6	8	8	1	☐
5	0	12	12	9	9	0	☐
6	0	12	12	10	10	2	☐

WWW.bodyADVANCE.COM

Recording Your "Energize" Regimen

Tap on Nutrition to record a part of your "energize" regimen.

Nutrition

Day:	Date:	Meal 1:
01	5/26/03	Hero sandwich – lite
02	5/27/03	
03	5/28/03	
04	5/29/03	
05	5/30/03	
06	5/31/03	
08	6/2/03	
09	6/3/03	

(Show) ▼ incomplete

WWW.bodyADVANCE.COM

Select the time of day for each meal. If a menu item is on the list, its proteins, calories, carbohydrates, and fat amounts will be added automatically.

Meals ▼ incomplete

Day: 01 Portions: protein: ▼ 3

Date: 5/26/03 carbs: ▼ 4

Time: 7:30 am vegs: ▼ 5

water: ▼ 8

eggs, cheese and a pattie

protein: 22.5 calories: 216

carbs: 6 fat: 9.3

WWW.bodyADVANCE.COM

Tap on Stretch and Rest to complete your energize regimen. Select the date and record the regimen.

Notes can be added each day.

Once you have recorded your nutrition and exercise levels, you can review your fitness plan further by doing the following:

- Try adding items to the menu. For example, what are your protein, calorie, carbohydrate, and fat counts? (Use the additional EatIt! application from www.schereronline.net/en/eatit/download.php for the Palm or Rational Nutrition for Pocket PC at www.hot-shareware.com/home-education/ rational-nutrition/)
- Which muscles are you using during your exercise? Identify them with a graphic display of muscles throughout your body. (Muxles at www .xenware.com/Muxles.htm for Palm or 3D Anatomy for Pocket at www .medicalpocketpc.com/for Pocket PC)

3. THE PICKLE POND STUDY

Overview and Learning Outcomes

After visiting a local pond, students design questions that relate to its water quality and discuss conditions that could change in the environment. Before collection of data with various sensors (e.g., temperature, light, pH, DO), the students predict possible findings. After the testing occurs, students compare their predictions to the data to answer their questions. This type of "science learning in context" provides an opportunity for students to question the impact on their environment of everyday phenomena such as pollution or ecotourism. By predicting outcomes of testing throughout the year on a local pond, students can further use inquiry skills to observe overall system changes resulting from the introduction of new circumstances that occur naturally, such as falling leaves, pollen, snow, or rain. This method of investigation allows students to develop further questions to study and helps them understand the relationships surrounding their natural environment. Research shows that with real-time data display, students can notice disparities in their measurements immediately and raise important questions about unexpected results or differences: What have I learned that could explain these differences? Are there any characteristics of this pond that would cause these differences? Are the probes not calibrated correctly? Should someone else verify my reading? In other words, students act like scientists, an occurrence that happens all too infrequently in the typical science classroom (SRI International & Palm, Inc., 2002).

Suggested Software Application

Palm OS: ImagiProbe and sensors with sensor interface by ImagiWorks (www.imagiworks.com)

Pocket PC: EasySense Flash and sensors with sensor interface by DataHarvest (www.dataharvest.com)

Grade Levels

This activity is appropriate for grade levels 2–12.

Standards

National Academies of Science

The following standards are from the National Academies of Science (1996) and can be found online at www.nap.edu/readingroom/books/nses/html/6d .html#csc58

- Science as Inquiry: Scientists formulate and test explanations of nature using observation, experiments, and theoretical and mathematical models
- Understanding About Scientific Inquiry: Technology used to gather data enhances accuracy and allows scientists to analyze and quantify results of investigations
- Life Science: Organisms and environments
- Life Science: Populations and ecosystems
- Life Science: Matter, energy, and organization in living systems
- Science in Personal and Social Perspectives: Populations, resources, and environments

National Council of Teachers of English

The following standards are from the National Council of Teachers of English (1998) and are available online at www.readwritethink.org/standards/

- Students conduct research on issues and interests by generating ideas and questions, and by posing problems. They gather, evaluate, and synthesize data from a variety of sources (e.g., print and nonprint texts, artifacts, people) to communicate their discoveries in ways that suit their purpose and audience
- Students use a variety of technological and information resources (e.g., libraries, databases, computer networks, video) to gather and synthesize information and to create and communicate knowledge
- Students use spoken, written, and visual language to accomplish their own purposes (e.g., for learning, enjoyment, persuasion, and the exchange of information)

International Society for Technology in Education

The following standards are from the International Society for Technology in Education (2000) and can be found online at http://cnets.iste.org/students/ s_stands.html

- Basic operations and concepts: Students are proficient in the use of technology
- Technology research tools: Students use technology tools to process data and report results

- Technology problem-solving and decision-making tools: Students employ technology in the development of strategies for solving problems in the real world

Designing the Investigation

Select ImagiProbe from the Launcher or Home.

Tap on the New Investigation button to open a folder file to contain all trials that relate to one specific location or equipment setting. In this example, students study a local body of water called Pickle Pond every 2 weeks throughout the school year.

Tap on the Investigation 1 box. A New Name box will appear. Place the name of your investigation on the line below. Enter a new name at the bottom of the screen.

Tap on the OK button. Tap on the New Trial button to set up your first data collection.

Investigation – ImagiProbe

Name: ⁝Pickle Pond⁝

Trials:

> No Trials created

(Back)   (New Trial)   ⊘

Tap on the Trial 1 button at the top of the screen to name the trial. Briefly describe the sensor(s) that will be used for the trial as the title. Tap the OK button.

Edit Trial Setup   ❶

Name: ⁝Trial 1⁝

Tap to choose a sensor:

❶ no sensor, no calibration
❷ no sensor, no calibration
❸ no sensor, no calibration
❹ no sensor, no calibration

New Name

Enter a new name:

Temperature

(OK) (Cancel)

Now it is time to assign the sensor and the sensor channel or location in the Edit Trial Setup. Because you are using only one sensor, you will tap on the first sensor (1) to assign the temperature sensor.

Choose Sensors   ❶

First pick a Sensor:
▼ no sensor
Then pick a Calibration:
▼ no calibration

❶ no sensor, no calibration
❷ no sensor, no calibration
❸ no sensor, no calibration
❹ no sensor, no calibration

(OK) (Cancel)

Tap on the "no sensor" option below First pick a Sensor submenu. Scroll through the types of sensors by using the arrow at the bottom right of the screen. Select Temp. DC (VST) from the list.

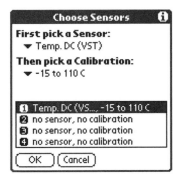

The calibration for this sensor will automatically appear on the screen. The calibration refers to sensors whose ranges have been interpolated to a given linear equation or two known values on a resulting linear plot.

If more than one sensor is needed, repeat this process. Each additional sensor add is assigned the next number based on the location at which the sensors are connected to the sensor interface attached to the handheld. This particular trial used only the −15 to 110C Temp sensor. Tap on the OK button if the selected calibration selection is acceptable. Tap on the Set Rate button to identify the sensor collection rate.

Tap on the Time unit submenu to select the timing of the sampling. For this study, the time unit is seconds.

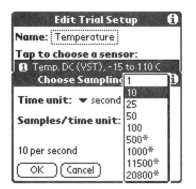

Tap on the Samples/Time unit submenu to select the frequency of collection. The collection rate can range between 1 and 20,800 sample(s) per time unit.

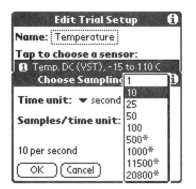

For this type of environmental study, the collection rate of 10 samples per second is appropriate. Tap on the OK button when finished.

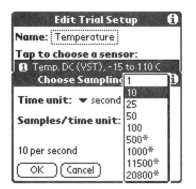

Tap on the OK button. A new Preview button will appear at the center of the bottom of the screen when the Edit Trial Setup is completed.

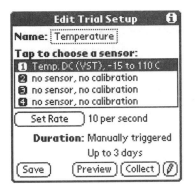

Attach the sensor interface to the handheld computer. The sensor interface interprets electrical current produced by a transducer found in the sensor into a number by electrical circuitry. Depending on the make and age of the handheld computer, the sensor interface will vary in shape, size, style, and position for sensor attachment. Attach the desired sensor to the connector and insert it into the sensor interface. Refer to the instructions provided with the sensor and sensor interface for exact instructions on how to connect to the handheld computer.

Designing the Trial

Before taking any measurements, carefully plan your study. Tap on the Notes button, shown as a pencil at the bottom right of the screen.

Select the Text tool on the bottom left of your screen to annotate your drawing. An empty Notes text box will appear on the screen immediately after you tap on the Notes button. Use an attachable keyboard, Graffiti™, or the pop-up keyboard on the screen to write your description and question(s).

```
┌──────────────────────────────┐
│     Notes – Temperature      │
│ ............................ │
│ ............................ │
│ ............................ │
│ ............................ │
│ ............................ │
│ ............................ │
│ ............................ │
│ ............................ │
│ ............................ │
│ ............................ │
│ ┌────────┐                   │
│ │  Done  │              ↑    │
│ └────────┘                   │
└──────────────────────────────┘
```

Record the weather conditions and describe the setting around your site. Consider a meaningful discovery question that will be answered by collecting data.

```
┌──────────────────────────────┐
│     Notes – Temperature      │
│ The temperature is chilly. The sky │
│ is overcast. The leaves are falling │
│ on the ground and into the water at │
│ the base of the tree at the side of │
│ the pond.                    │
│ Some of the water is protected │
│ from the cold by the new leaves │
│ that have fallen.            │
│ Is the water temperature at the │
│ surface the same as at the   │
│ bottom?                      │
│ ┌────────┐                   │
│ │  Done  │                   │
│ └────────┘                   │
└──────────────────────────────┘
```

Predict the results of your trial data collection. State the justification for your reasoning.

```
┌──────────────────────────────┐
│     Notes – Temperature      │
│ I predict that the temperature is  ▲ │
│ colder at the bottom of the pond,  ▓ │
│ since heat rises. I think that the ▓ │
│ temperature would be the same at   ▓ │
│ the middle and the top since little ▓ │
│ cold can enter the pond due to the ▓ │
│ leaves.                      │
│                              │
│ It is the end of October and the │
│ temperatures are freezing on the │
│ ground at night.             ▼ │
│ ┌────────┐                   │
│ │  Done  │                   │
│ └────────┘                   │
└──────────────────────────────┘
```

Once that step is completed, tap on the Done button to return to the Edit Trial Setup.

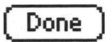

Collecting Data

Tap on the Preview button to view a sample of initial measurements, displayed in metric and graphical form.

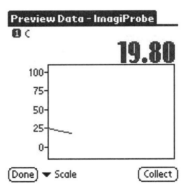

Once you are comfortable with the data display, tap on the Collect button to record measurements.

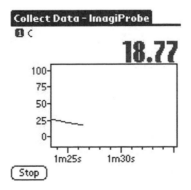

Based on your discovery question, place the sensor in the appropriate location(s) to test your hypothesis. After the procedure is finished, tap on the Stop button.

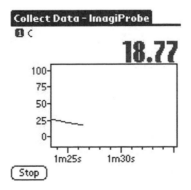

If you are satisfied with your methods of collecting the data, tap on the Stop button.

Tap on the Done button when you are finished reviewing the data.

Tap on the Back button to return to the Trial list.

Analyzing the Data

You can reselect your trial from the investigation folder to again review the data, or you can decide to start another trial.

Trial – ImagiProbe

Name: Temperature

Sensors chosen:
  Temp. DC (VST), -15 to 110 C

Sample Rate: 10 per second
Duration: Manually triggered
  2m25s

(Back)   (View Data)   (⊘)

You can review your entire dataset by using the tools at the bottom of the graph. You can change the scale or move systematically through a large dataset by using the arrows.

Once you have analyzed the results of your study, tap on the Note button to describe the conclusion of the trial. Tap on Done when finished.

Return to the investigation folder to design additional trials that will help you further answer your discovery question.

Manipulating and   5
Displaying Data

Because many new technologies are interactive, it is now easier to create environments in which students can learn by doing, receive feedback, and continually refine their understanding and build new knowledge (National Research Council, 1999). Handheld technology makes it possible for students to see data represented symbolically in ways that greatly increase comprehension and process skills. Research has shown that while students use the various pieces of handheld software, their learning is enhanced by moving among the multiple representations (e.g., concept maps, text documents, pictures, and animations) of the content (Norris & Soloway, 2003).

When students manipulate two functions simultaneously on the same graph, they can compare changes in coefficients, slopes, intercepts, and other measures. Although this type of investigation is not new in classrooms that use graphing calculators, a teacher with handhelds in the classroom can now go a step further and test student understanding. Students can explain the patterns and terms in their own words in the Notes section of their handhelds before infrared beaming their definitions to other students (and the teacher) for peer review (Staudt, 2002a).

The concept of motion—the rate of change of distance and velocity over time—is a difficult topic for students to understand. Making mathematics come alive by representing motion in a graphical form is fundamental to enhancing understanding of this phenomenon. Ron Thornton of Tufts University is one of the leading educational researchers studying student models of motion by using a sonar transceiver or motion sensor, which can also be attached to a handheld computer. By using their own bodies to produce a motion graph while walking, stopping, or running with the motion sensor, students can visualize their speed and acceleration. As Thornton states:

> There is evidence that listening to someone talk about scientific facts and results is not an effective means of developing concepts. The

evidence shows that students of all ages learn science better by actively participating in the investigation and the interpretation of physical phenomena and that well-designed computer-based pedagogical tools that make it possible for students to gather, analyze, visualize, model and communicate data can aid students who are actively working to understand science. (Thornton, 1999)

Beyond this, students can further manipulate simulated motion graphs effectively on the handheld computer to understand the true meanings of how a distance versus time graph can be equated to its derivative, a velocity versus time graph.

Besides demonstrating the use of a graphing program to display and compare functions and the manipulation of graphs in a simulation, one of the following activities shows the effective display of data in the form of a searchable database. Just as doctors often utilize medical databases to study the rapidly advancing literature and reports of case studies, students can design and build a field guide to track local environmental changes.

1. FREQUENT SINES

Overview and Learning Outcomes

Students manipulate and compare sine waves to discover equations that increase and decrease their frequency. Graphs convey particular kinds of information visually, whereas symbolic expressions may be easier for students to manipulate, analyze, and transform. By predicting and exploring their own rules, students are able to verbalize and communicate math by testing their models.

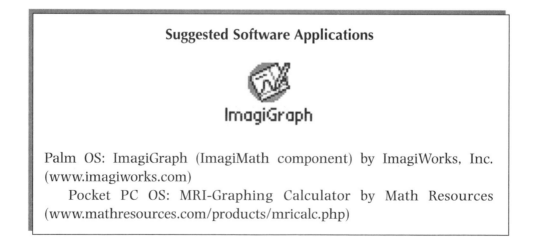

Suggested Software Applications

ImagiGraph

Palm OS: ImagiGraph (ImagiMath component) by ImagiWorks, Inc. (www.imagiworks.com)

Pocket PC OS: MRI-Graphing Calculator by Math Resources (www.mathresources.com/products/mricalc.php)

Grade Levels

This activity is appropriate for grade levels 5–12.

Standards

National Council of Teachers of Mathematics

The following standards are from the National Council of Teachers of Mathematics (2000) and can be found online at www.standards.nctm.org/document/chapter1/index.htm

- Algebra: Understand patterns, relations, and functions
- Algebra: Use mathematical models to represent and understand quantitative relationships
- Measurement: Apply appropriate techniques, tools, and formulas to determine measurements
- Data Analysis and Probability: Formulate questions that can be addressed with data and collect, organize, and display relevant data to answer them
- Data Analysis and Probability: Develop and evaluate inferences and predictions that are based on data
- Problem Solving: Solve problems that arise in mathematics and in other contexts
- Communication: Communicate mathematical thinking coherently and clearly to peers, teachers, and others
- Connections: Recognize and apply mathematics in contexts outside of mathematics

National Academies of Science

The following standards are from the National Academies of Science (1996) and can be found online at www.nap.edu/readingroom/books/nses/html/6d.html#csc58

- Science as Inquiry: Scientists formulate and test explanations of nature using observation, experiments, and theoretical and mathematical models
- Understanding About Scientific Inquiry: Technology used to gather data enhances accuracy and allows scientists to analyze and quantify results of investigations
- Physical Science: Transfer of energy
- Physical Science: Interactions of energy and matter

National Council of Teachers of English

The following standards are from the National Council of Teachers of English (1998) and are available online at www.readwritethink.org/standards/

- Students conduct research on issues and interests by generating ideas and questions, and by posing problems. They gather, evaluate, and synthesize data from a variety of sources (e.g., print and nonprint texts, artifacts, people) to communicate their discoveries in ways that suit their purpose and audience.
- Students use spoken, written, and visual language to accomplish their own purposes (e.g., for learning, enjoyment, persuasion, and the exchange of information).

International Society for Technology in Education

The following standards are from the International Society for Technology in Education (2000) and can be found online at http://cnets.iste.org/students/s_stands.html

- Basic operations and concepts: Students are proficient in the use of technology.
- Technology research tools: Students use technology tools to process data and report results.
- Technology problem-solving and decision-making tools: Students employ technology in the development of strategies for solving problems in the real world.

Displaying Graphs

Select ImagiGraph from the Launcher or Home. When it opens, it will display an empty graphing space.

To define your first graph, tap on the arrow next to the red square.

When you select the New button, an Equation Editor will open. Tap on the description of your equation.

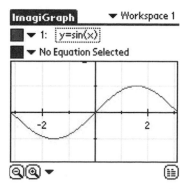

Tap OK to display the graph. Note the size and shape of the graph. How often does the graph cross the horizontal axis? Is there a consistent pattern to the sine wave?

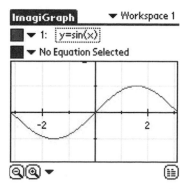

Create a second equation that will increase the frequency of the repeated sine wave. Is it possible to do this without increasing the height (amplitude) of the wave?

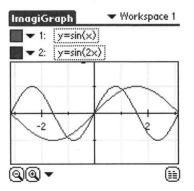

Analyzing the Graph

Once both sine waves are plotted, you can zoom out to observe more of the repeated patterns.

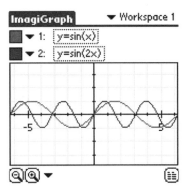

You can also tap on each sine wave to view coordinates of any one point.

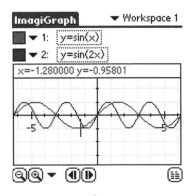

Select Notes from the Edit menu.

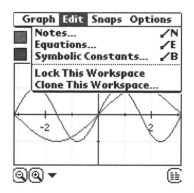

In the Notes, describe in words the differences between the two equations and their resulting graphs. How are the patterns of the sine waves similar? How does this pattern relate to the difference between the two equations? Can you state a rule that describes the increase in the frequency of the sine wave?

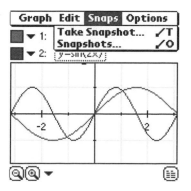

Testing Your Rule

Capture a screen shot of your two sine waves by selecting Take Snapshot from the Snaps menu.

Once you have named your Snapshot, you will be able to view it and beam it at any time by returning to the Snaps menu and selecting Snapshots.

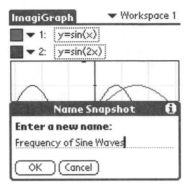

To test the rule you recorded in Notes, tap on the arrow next to the second equation and select New.

Try writing an equation for your rule by substituting the symbol "n" for the real number in the equation. This will enable you to view an animation of a series of graphs created by increasing the value of "n" in subsequent steps.

Select Animation Setup from the Graph menu. Based on the number of steps you choose, select the starting and ending value for n. Tap on OK.

To view the animation, tap on the Start arrow. How does the series of graphs display your rule?

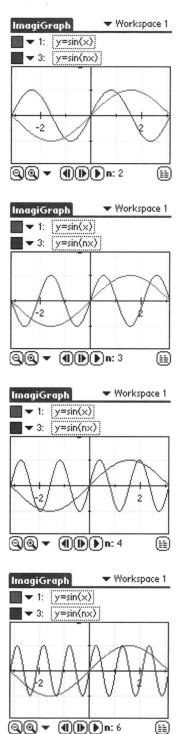

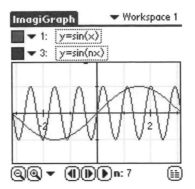

Tap on Workspace 1 on the top right of the screen and tap on Rename.

Enter a name that will remind you of the graph and animation so that you can find them later and share them with others by tapping on Beam.

Try answering the following questions by reviewing your graph:

- How would you decrease the frequency without changing the amplitude of the sine wave? (Display the graph, take a Snapshot, and write a rule in Notes.)

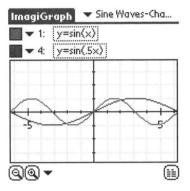

- How would you increase the amplitude without changing the frequency of the sine wave? (Display the graph, take a Snapshot, and write a rule in Notes.)

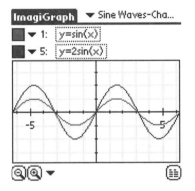

Extension: Use a tuning fork and a microphone sensor to demonstrate the change in frequency and amplitude of various sounds.

2. RATE OF CHANGE

Overview and Learning Outcomes

Students investigate and begin mastering precalculus concepts, including the meanings of position and velocity-time graphs and the relationship between slope and rate. Students predict and test their ideas about motion in meaningful contexts through animations and graphs developed for middle school students by the SimCalc project.

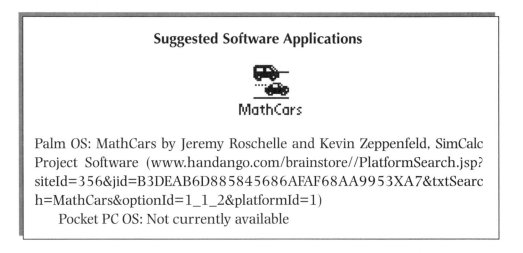

Suggested Software Applications

MathCars

Palm OS: MathCars by Jeremy Roschelle and Kevin Zeppenfeld, SimCalc Project Software (www.handango.com/brainstore//PlatformSearch.jsp?siteId=356&jid=B3DEAB6D885845686AFAF68AA9953XA7&txtSearch=MathCars&optionId=1_1_2&platformId=1)
        Pocket PC OS: Not currently available

Grade Levels

This activity is appropriate for grade levels 5–12.

Standards

National Council of Teachers of Mathematics

The following standards are from the National Council of Teachers of Mathematics (2000) and can be found online at www.standards.nctm.org/document/chapter1/index.htm

- Algebra: Understand patterns, relations, and functions
- Algebra: Use mathematical models to represent and understand quantitative relationships
- Algebra: Analyze change in various contexts
- Measurement: Apply appropriate techniques, tools, and formulas to determine measurements
- Data Analysis and Probability: Formulate questions that can be addressed with data and collect, organize, and display relevant data to answer them
- Data Analysis and Probability: Develop and evaluate inferences and predictions that are based on data
- Problem Solving: Solve problems that arise in mathematics and in other contexts

- Communication: Communicate mathematical thinking coherently and clearly to peers, teachers, and others
- Connections: Recognize and apply mathematics in contexts outside of mathematics

National Academies of Science

The following standards are from the National Academies of Science (1996) and can be found online at www.nap.edu/readingroom/books/nses/html/6d.html#csc58

- Science as Inquiry: Scientists formulate and test explanations of nature using observation, experiments, and theoretical and mathematical models
- Understanding About Scientific Inquiry: Technology used to gather data enhances accuracy and allows scientists to analyze and quantify results of investigations
- Physical Science: Motion and forces

International Society for Technology in Education

The following standards are from the International Society for Technology in Education (2000) and can be found online at http://cnets.iste.org/ students/ s_stands.html

- Basic operations and concepts: Students are proficient in the use of technology.
- Technology research tools: Students use technology tools to process data and report results.
- Technology problem-solving and decision-making tools: Students employ technology in the development of strategies for solving problems in the real world.

Exploring Motion

Select MathCars from the Launcher or Home.

Select Explore from the menu in the upper right corner.

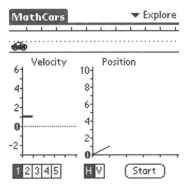

Tap on the Start button and explore how fast the car moves in a horizontal direction for each velocity graph. Is there a relationship between how fast the car is moving and the slope (lean) of the line?

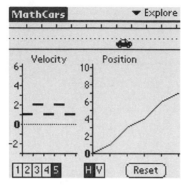

Tap and drag on the position of the line in the Velocity graph to position 4 by dragging the line from the location that intersects with the *y*-axis. How does the original position of the car change on the track?

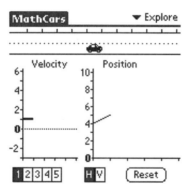

Repeat the five trials. What was the difference in motion between starting at 0 on the track and at 4 on the track?

Switch to the Vertical direction and view a vertical elevator rise instead of a horizontal track. How does the velocity of the elevator change with Velocity 1 through 5?

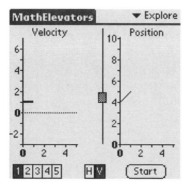

Try to find three different ways to get an elevator to rise to the sixth floor using any velocity graph. Use the Reset button to try another method. What remains the same in each of the three motions, and what is different?

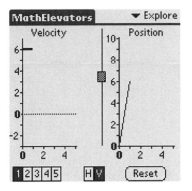

Comparing Motion

Select Apply from the menu in the upper right corner.

Switch to the Horizontal direction.

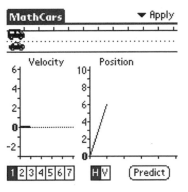

Try matching the velocity graph with the position graph. The velocity graph corresponds to the motion of the truck on the top of the screen, and the position graph corresponds to the motion of the car. While the Predict button is displayed on the bottom of the screen, you can tap on the ends of the position lines and move them to a new location and even change the lean of the line. Tap on the Predict button to continue.

Test out your prediction by tapping on the Start button.

If your prediction is correct, you will see a happy face at the top of the screen. If your prediction is incorrect, you will see an unhappy face.

If you wish to try again, tap on the Reset button to move the vehicles back to their original positions.

Tap on the Try Again button to make another attempt to match the motions of the vehicles.

For example, in Level 1, the following sequence shows several attempts before a match was found.

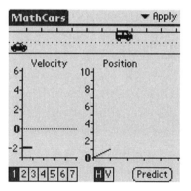

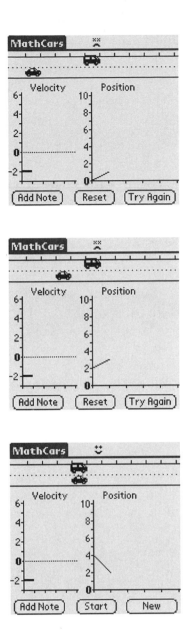

After finding a match, enter a note describing the method that you used to make the two vehicles display the same motion. Tap on the Add Note button and write a short description. Tap on Done to close the note.

Continue completing several matches for each level by tapping on the New button.

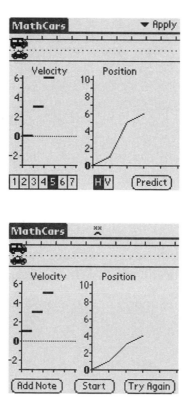

Once you are successful on a certain level, you will be given a chance to select a new and more difficult level by tapping on a higher level. This is an example of several Level 5 attempts.

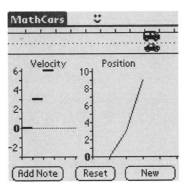

Switch to the Vertical direction and view two vertical elevators.

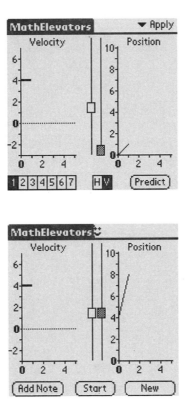

After completing each level for both the horizontal and vertical direction, answer the following questions:

- How did a horizontal velocity line relate to a position line?
- How did the length and lean of a position line relate to a velocity line?
- How did a positive or negative position line relate to the location of a velocity line on the axis?

3. FIELD GUIDE

Overview and Learning Outcomes

Students design and build a diversified field guide to their local environment. They develop an understanding of relationships among organisms and their physical environment. Students gather information about biological adaptation and diversity of life. By developing a database of their local environment, students recognize the use of technology to help capture, organize, and track environmental change over time.

Suggested Software Applications

Palm OS: SmartList To Go by DataViz (http://dataviz.com/smartlistogo)
Pocket PC: FileMaker Mobile by FileMaker, Inc. (www.filemaker.com/products/mbl_home.html)

Grade Levels

This activity is appropriate for grade levels 2–12.

Standards

National Academies of Science

The following standards are from the National Academies of Science (1996) and can be found online at www.nap.edu/readingroom/books/nses/html/6d.html#csc58

- Science as Inquiry: Scientists formulate and test explanations of nature using observation, experiments, and theoretical and mathematical models
- Understanding About Scientific Inquiry: Technology used to gather data enhances accuracy and allows scientists to analyze and quantify results of investigations

- Life Science: Organisms and environments
- Life Science: Populations and ecosystems
- Life Science: Matter, energy, and organization in living systems
- Science in Personal and Social Perspectives: Populations, resources, and environments

National Council of Teachers of English

The following standards are from the National Council of Teachers of English (1998) and are available online at www.readwritethink.org/standards/

- Students conduct research on issues and interests by generating ideas and questions, and by posing problems. They gather, evaluate, and synthesize data from a variety of sources (e.g., print and nonprint texts, artifacts, people) to communicate their discoveries in ways that suit their purpose and audience.
- Students use spoken, written, and visual language to accomplish their own purposes (e.g., for learning, enjoyment, persuasion, and the exchange of information).

International Society for Technology in Education

The following standards are from the International Society for Technology in Education (2000) and can be found online at http://cnets.iste.org/students/s_stands.html

- Basic operations and concepts: Students are proficient in the use of technology.
- Technology research tools: Students use technology tools to process data and report results.
- Technology problem-solving and decision-making tools: Students employ technology in the development of strategies for solving problems in the real world.

Creating Your Field Guide

Select SmartList from the Launcher or Home.

Tap on the SmartList To Go header and select Create New SmartList.

Enter your title and select Define on the screen.

```
┌────────────────────────────────┐
│     SmartList Properties       │
├────────────────────────────────┤
│ SmartList: Field Guide         │
│                                │
│  ☐ SmartList is read-only      │
│                                │
│  ☑ Search when doing Global Find│
│                                │
│  ☐ Do NOT backup during HotSync │
│ Startup Screen: ( Define... )  │
│ ( OK )  ( Cancel )             │
└────────────────────────────────┘
```

Enter a description that will explain your database to a new user. Tap on OK twice when finished.

```
┌────────────────────────────────┐
│  About this SmartList    ❶     │
├────────────────────────────────┤
│ Identifying the diversity in the│
│ local forest.                  │
│ ...............................│
│ ...............................│
│ ...............................│
│ ...............................│
│ ...............................│
│ ...............................│
│ ...............................│
│ ...............................│
│ ( OK )   ☑ Show this screen    │
│              at startup        │
└────────────────────────────────┘
```

To enable this description to be seen by every new user, tap on the box selection that will show this screen at startup.

```
┌────────────────────────────────┐
│  About this SmartList    ❶     │
├────────────────────────────────┤
│ Field Guide                    │
│                                │
│ Identifying the diversity in the│
│ local forest.                  │
│                                │
│                                │
│                                │
│                                │
│                                │
│ ( OK )   ☑ Show this screen    │
│              at startup        │
└────────────────────────────────┘
```

Select Design Fields by tapping on the Design Tool at the bottom of the screen or from the Tools menu.

List all the items (fields) that you would like to check while out in the field. Tap on the Type submenu next to each field to identify the kind of description you would like to assign to each. Scroll through all the options by tapping on the arrow.

For example, the Radio Button option provides a series of choices. Tap on the Done button when finished adding options.

A variety of types of fields can be used within the field guide. Tap on the Done button when finished.

Completing the Field Guide

Tap on the New Record icon at the bottom of the screen to fill out a record of a site in your field guide.

Complete each field. Write or select a date from a calendar (or alternatively, simply tap on the Today button for the present date).

Enter a time (or simply tap on the Now button for the present time).

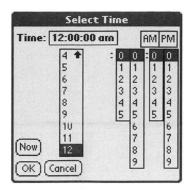

Tap on Site description and write about your site. Tap on the OK button when finished.

Select the leaf type (or other object of study) by clicking on the radio button choice that best fits the leaf type.

Tap on drawing to draw a picture of what you observed at the site. Tap on the OK button when finished.

Reviewing the Sites

After visiting any of the sites, you can select Reports/Statistics to see an overview of each one of the characteristics recorded. Use the pull-down menu to select the characteristic you would like to review.

```
╔════════════════════════════════╗
│ SmartList To Go        ▼ none  │
│ Statistics for: ▼ Type of leaf │
│    Apply filter: ▼ none        │
│ ┌──── Results ────┐            │
│ Fir                         1  │
│ Deciduous                   0  │
│ Both                        1  │
│ Neither                     1  │
│ No Type of leaf             0  │
│                                │
│                                │
│ ( Done )    ▦    Σ %           │
╚════════════════════════════════╝
```

In some cases, it may be beneficial to find the percentage of one type of site and perhaps compare it to the percentage of another.

```
╔════════════════════════════════╗
│ SmartList To Go        ▼ none  │
│ Statistics for: ▼ Type of leaf │
│    Apply filter: ▼ none        │
│ ┌──── Results ────┐            │
│ Fir                     33.3%  │
│ Deciduous                0.0%  │
│ Both                    33.3%  │
│ Neither                 33.3%  │
│ No Type of leaf          0.0%  │
│                                │
│                                │
│ ( Done )    ▦    Σ %           │
╚════════════════════════════════╝
```

By selecting Design Forms from the Tools menu, you can change the look of your report for each site.

```
╔════════════════════════════════╗
│ SmartList  Tools  About        │
│ ▼ F│ Design Fields...      ╱F  │
│ Dat│ Design Forms...       ╱O  │
│ 6/: │ Design Views...       ╱V  │
│  5. │ Design Filters...     ╱L  │
│ 6/: │ Design Lists...       ╱I  │
│    ┊┈┈┈┈┈┈┈┈┈┈┈┈┈┈┈┈┈┈┈       │
│     Find...               ╱1  │
│     Filtered Operations... │
│     Reports/Statistics... ╱E  │
│     Print / Export...     ╱W  │
│     Auto-Size All Columns  │
│    ┄┄┄┄┄┄┄┄┄┄┄┄┄┄┄┄┄┄┄       │
│     Preferences...        ╱R  │
│ 🏠 □ ▥ ▐ ⊠ ↲          4/4  │
╚════════════════════════════════╝
```

Tap on each empty box to select the field that you would like to show.

By selecting Design Views from the Tools menu, you can also sort the categories within your field guide.

Collaborating on a Field Guide

Tap on the Home icon at the bottom of the screen to view and select your field guide.

With your field guide selected, you can beam it to others to share the format.

How do other sites compare to yours? (Once others have recorded the characteristics of their sites, they can beam their records back to you for review by tapping on the Actions menu from within their record.)

Communicating   6
and Collaborating

T he workplace is built on teaming and cooperation between members of teams that communicate ideas effectively to justify a position, persuade and convince others, resolve divergent ideas, and work toward agreements involving exchanges of resources (U.S. Department of Labor, Employment & Training Administration, 1991). To cope with the demands of the 21st century, students need to demonstrate teamwork and leadership, to adapt to varied roles and responsibilities, to work productively with others, to exercise empathy, and to respect diverse perspectives (Partnership for 21st Century Skills, 2002). Promoting the development of these skills in schools is paramount in creating a workforce that can meet the needs of a technologically connected world.

As part of the 1999 software competition sponsored by the Center for Innovative Learning Technologies for the development of educational software, focus for the winning entries was placed on using the unique features provided by a handheld environment. One of the most exceptional features is the capability of the devices to easily transfer data wirelessly through infrared beaming. Geney (http://geney.juxta.com/) won the overall competition, with software that made it possible for students to select two virtual fish to breed in a "pond" that resided on their handheld computer. After glimpsing the offspring's genetic code, students could beam it to another handheld computer if they did not want it in their pond. (The present rendition of the application has alien Zwiki creatures that need to breed a specific genetic strand to go back to their galaxy.) This type of participatory application makes it possible for students to solve problems collaboratively with others. Additional participatory simulations involving shared survival techniques are being developed by the Massachusetts Institute of Technology (http://education.mit.edu/pda/games.htm). These include Big Fish–Little Fish, Live Long and Prosper, Tit for Tat, Sugar and Spice, and Virus.

At present, most handheld computer applications allow students to beam data between devices, in the form of text, graphs, and pictures. Some of the applications focus on the sharing of data for completion of a project. These types of collaborative applications include the creation of project plans among individual team members to report and track progress of overall group work, the joint writing of a shared story among team members, and the design of a joint concept map to brainstorm and elaborate relationships and main points of an idea. As wireless components become more cost-effective and, as a result, more available, collaborative white boards will be used to share ideas between more than two people at the same time.

1. VIKING TIMES PROJECT

Overview and Learning Outcomes

Student teams plan times, formulate tasks, and monitor the completion of a class project. By organizing the various aspects of the project in advance, students define the levels of complexity and the research and development needed to complete the study of a historical Viking era. Students also track progress throughout the project and learn how to manage time.

Suggested Software Application

Palm OS: Project@Hand™ by Natara Software (www.natara.com/ ProjectAtHand/index.cfm)

Pocket PC: Pocket Plan by Twiddlebit (www.twiddlebit.com/ products.htm)

Grade Levels

This activity is appropriate for grade levels 5–12.

Standards

National Center for History in the Schools

The following standards are from the National Center for History in the Schools (1996) and can be found online at http://www.sscnet.ucla.edu/ nchs/standards

- Chronological Thinking: Compare alternative models for periodization by identifying the organizing principles on which each is based.
- Historical Comprehension: Appreciate historical perspectives—(a) describing the past on its own terms, through the eyes and experiences of those who were there, as revealed through their literature, diaries, letters, debates, arts, artifacts, and the like; (b) considering the historical context in which the event unfolded—the values, outlook, options, and contingencies of that time and place; and (c) avoiding "present-mindedness," judging the past solely in terms of present-day norms and values.
- Historical Analysis and Interpretation: Consider multiple perspectives of various peoples in the past by demonstrating their differing motives, beliefs, interests, hopes, and fears.
- Historical Research Capabilities: Obtain historical data from a variety of sources, including library and museum collections, historic sites, historical photos, journals, diaries, eyewitness accounts, newspapers, and the like; documentary films, oral testimony from living witnesses, censuses, tax records, city directories, statistical compilations, and economic indicators.
- Historical Issues Analysis and Decision Making: Identify issues and problems in the past and analyze the interests, values, perspectives, and points of view of those involved in the situation.

National Council for the Social Studies

The following standards are from the National Council for the Social Studies (1994) and are available online at www.ncss.org/standards/toc.html/

- Culture: Experiences that provide for the study of culture and cultural diversity
- Time, Continuity and Change: Experiences that provide for the study of the ways human beings view themselves in and over time
- People, Places and Environments: Experiences that provide for the study of people, places, and environments
- Production, Distribution and Consumption: Experiences that provide for the study of how people organize for the production, distribution, and consumption of goods and services

International Society for Technology in Education

The following standards are from the International Society for Technology in Education (2000) and can be found online at http://cnets.iste.org/students/s_stands.html

- Basic operations and concepts: Students are proficient in the use of technology.

- Technology productivity tools: Students use productivity tools to collaborate in constructing technology-enhanced models, prepare publications, and produce other creative works.
- Technology research tools: Students use technology, to locate, evaluate, and collect information from a variety of sources.

Defining the Research

Select Project@Hand from the Launcher or Home.

Tap on the New button to name your project.

Set the starting date by tapping on the calendar.

Tap on the Task icon at the bottom of the screen to enter a task for the completion of the project.

Enter the task by typing into the highlighted area for the Task name. Enter the finishing date by tapping on the appropriate box and selecting the date from the calendar. Adjust the finishing date according to the instructions on the screen that fit your project. In this case, Finish No Earlier Than (FNET) fits the project. Tap on the OK button when finished.

Add the major tasks that are needed to research the project.

Tap on the Define Task tool at the bottom of the screen to further describe the tasks.

Tap on the Resource tab to add any additional resources (e.g., people, texts, Web sites) for references during your research.

Tap on the Add button to list the resources and tap on the OK button. Tap on the OK button again to add the first resource.

Type in the name and initials of the new resource and tap on the OK button twice when finished.

```
┌─────────────────────────────────────┐
│   Research exploration      ❶        │
│ ┌─────────────────────────────────┐ │
│ │      New Resource       ❶       │ │
│ │  Name:  Museum of Science       │ │
│ │ Initials:  MS                   │ │
│ │   Type:   ▼ Work                │ │
│ │   Rate:  ........ per hour      │ │
│ │   Cost:  ........ per use       │ │
│ │ Max Units:  100  %              │ │
│ │                                 │ │
│ │                                 │ │
│ │  ( OK )  ( Cancel )       ♣     │ │
│ └─────────────────────────────────┘ │
└─────────────────────────────────────┘
```

Continue to list your resources for each task.

After highlighting the first task, tap again on the Define Task tool at the bottom of the screen. Select the Notes tab.

```
┌─────────────────────────────────────┐
│    Research exploration             │
│ [General|Resource|Pred|Adv|Notes|   │
│ │                               │   │
│ │                               │   │
│ │                               │   │
│ │                               │   │
│ │                               │   │
│ │                               │   │
│ │                               │   │
│ │                               │   │
│ │  ( OK ) ( Cancel )            │   │
│ └───────────────────────────────┘   │
└─────────────────────────────────────┘
```

Write the specific task that must be completed in the specified time for this research group.

```
┌─────────────────────────────────────┐
│    Research exploration             │
│ [General|Resource|Pred|Adv|Notes|   │
│ Draw a map of the Viking            │
│ explorations throughout             │
│ Scandinavia.                        │
│                                     │
│                                     │
│                                     │
│                                     │
│                                     │
│  ( OK ) ( Cancel )                  │
└─────────────────────────────────────┘
```

Complete notes for each research group.

Defining the Product

Highlight the first research task and tap on the Task icon at the bottom of the screen. Title this task and set the time period for completion.

```
┌──────────────────────────────┐
│      Viking journal       ⓘ  │
│ ┌─────┬────────┬────┬───┬─────┐│
│ │General│Resource│Pred│Adv│Notes││
│ Viking journal               │
│ ······························ │
│ ······························ │
│  Duration: 7      ▼ Day(s)   │
│  Complete: 0   %  [____]     │
│   Priority: 500              │
│                              │
│   Start:  10/20/03   8:00 am │
│   Finish: 10/28/03   5:00 pm │
│  ( OK )( Cancel )            │
└──────────────────────────────┘
```

Because these tasks are completed after the research, select the Predecessor tab to set the dependency on the research.

```
┌──────────────────────────────┐
│      Viking journal       ⓘ  │
│ ┌─────┬────────┬────┬───┬─────┐│
│ │General│Resource│Pred│Adv│Notes││
│ Task Name              Type  │
│ ┌──────────────────────────┐ │
│ │                          │ │
│ │                          │ │
│ │                          │ │
│ │                          │ │
│ └──────────────────────────┘ │
│  ( Add )( Details )( Remove )│
│  ( OK )( Cancel )            │
└──────────────────────────────┘
```

Highlight and select the research that relates to the task. Tap on the OK button when finished.

```
┌──────────────────────────────┐
│    Select Predecessor     ⓘ  │
│ Task                         │
│ 1 Research exploration       │
│ 3 Research religion          │
│ 4 Religious jewelry          │
│ 5 Research farming and food  │
│ 6 Viking meal                │
│ 7 Research ship building     │
│ 8 Build a longship        ↓  │
│ Type: ▼ Finish-to-Start (FS) │
│   Lag: 0      ▼ Day(s)       │
│  ( OK )( Cancel )            │
└──────────────────────────────┘
```

Tap on the Notes tab and enter the required product specifics.

Viking journal

| General | Resource | Pred | Adv | Notes |

Write a daily journal of a viking oarsman as he works on the longboat on the way to Persia or China.

(OK) (Cancel)

Enter a product task for each research group within notes.

Completing the Project

Every day, enter each research task and identify the task completion by listing the percentage or using the slider to show the amount completed. Tap on the OK button when finished with each research task.

Research exploration ℹ

| General | Resource | Pred | Adv | Notes |

Research exploration

Duration: 7 ▼ Day(s)
Complete: 34 %
Priority: 500

Start: 10/13/03 | 8:00 am
Finish: 10/21/03 | 5:00 pm
(OK) (Cancel)

For an overview of the project, tap on the Gantt Chart icon at the bottom of the screen.

Viking Times ▼ All Tasks

11/2003

- Research exploration
- ↳ Viking journal
- Research religion
- ↳ Religious jewelry
- Research farming and food
- ↳ Viking meal
- Research ship building
- ↳ Build a longship
- Research law and government
- ↳ Viking trial

Observe your progress and scroll through the entire project by using the arrows at the bottom of the screen. Notice that the black lines denote completion of the research to date.

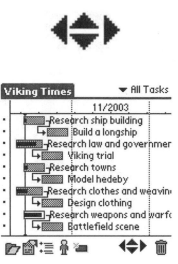

Depending on the date and the amount of completed research, the project team should meet on a regular basis to review progress and shortcomings. If additional resources or assistance have been identified, they should be entered into the project plan.

2. LOST TRIBES OF AMAZON

Overview and Learning Outcomes

Students develop a decision tree with alternate paths of action for a particular topic of concern (for example, a student considers the lost tribes of the Amazon in the sample activity here). By proposing and defending different choices, students analyze a variety of positions or sides. Students use general skills and strategies of the writing process while presenting their case in a short narrative. After sharing decision trees with one another by beaming, other students can agree, elaborate, refute, or add alternatives.

Suggested Software Application

WIB

Palm OS: What-If Builder by KidSolve™, Inc. (original desktop version developed at The Concord Consortium) (www.kidsolve.com/products/palm/wib/index.html)
    Pocket PC: Available soon

Grade Levels

This activity is appropriate for grade levels 3–12.

Standards

The following standards are from the National Council of Teachers of English (1998) and are available online at www.readwritethink.org/standards/

- Students apply a wide range of strategies to comprehend, interpret, evaluate, and appreciate texts. They draw on their prior experience, their interactions with other readers and writers, their knowledge of word meaning and of other texts, their word identification strategies, and their understanding of textual features (e.g., sound-letter correspondence, sentence structure, context, graphics).
- Students employ a wide range of strategies as they write and use different writing process elements appropriately to communicate with different audiences for a variety of purposes.
- Students conduct research on issues and interests by generating ideas and questions, and by posing problems. They gather, evaluate, and synthesize data from a variety of sources (e.g., print and nonprint texts, artifacts, people) to communicate their discoveries in ways that suit their purpose and audience.
- Students use a variety of technological and information resources (e.g., libraries, databases, computer networks, video) to gather and synthesize information and to create and communicate knowledge.
- Students use spoken, written, and visual language to accomplish their own purposes (e.g., for learning, enjoyment, persuasion, and the exchange of information).

National Council for the Social Studies

The following standards are from the National Council for the Social Studies (1994) and are available online at www.ncss.org/standards/toc.html/

- Culture: Experiences that provide for the study of culture and cultural diversity
- Time, Continuity and Change: Experiences that provide for the study of the ways human beings view themselves in and over time
- People, Places and Environments: Experiences that provide for the study of people, places, and environments

International Society for Technology in Education

The following standards are from the International Society for Technology in Education (2000) and can be found online at http://cnets.iste.org/students/s_stands.html

- Basic operations and concepts: Students are proficient in the use of technology.
- Social, ethical, and human issues: Students understand the ethical, cultural, and societal issues related to technology.
- Technology research tools: Students use technology tools to process data and report results.
- Technology problem-solving and decision-making tools: Students use technology resources for solving problems and making informed decisions.
- Technology problem-solving and decision-making tools: Students employ technology in the development of strategies for solving problems in the real world.

Defining the Scenario

Select WIB from the Launcher or Home.

Tap on the New button to name your story.

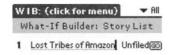

Tap on the GO button to describe the basis for your story in the Page View. This short narrative is the major premise of your story and will provide you with options for future discussion or debate.

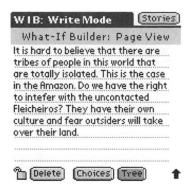

Select the Choices button at the bottom of the screen to enter options. In the case of the Lost Tribes of Amazon, the student felt only two choices of action existed: lead expeditions into the Amazon or prevent all contact with the Indians.

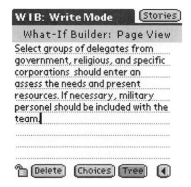

Once the choices have been listed, tap on the GO button to elaborate further on each option in a narrative format in the Page View.

```
WIB: Write Mode        [Stories]
  What-If Builder: Page View
Boundaries with no-cross zones
should be established so the the
indians are left alone. Nieither
contact or materials should cross
the line. Once intervention occurs,
the relationship is compromised.

 [Delete]  [Choices] [Tree]  [◄]
```

Each choice provides an opportunity for the student to cite and elaborate on ramifications that are a direct result of each option.

```
WIB: Write Mode        [Stories]
   What-If Builder: Choices

1  Find a new cancer drug      [GO]
2  Obtain large amount of trees [GO]
   for building and furniture
3  Help the indians with our   [GO]
   medical knowledge

 [New] [Delete] [Tree] [Exit]
```

```
WIB: Write Mode        [Stories]
   What-If Builder: Choices

1  Prevent new (introduced     [GO]
   from outside) diseases
   among the lost tribes
2  Save the land and its animals [GO]
   from outside exploitation
3  Preserve the culture without [GO]
   "Coca Cola" being introduced

 [New] [Delete] [Tree] [Exit]
```

Creating a Decision Tree

As the options and their results become clear, students develop a decision tree that provides ample opportunity for discussion and debate among peers.

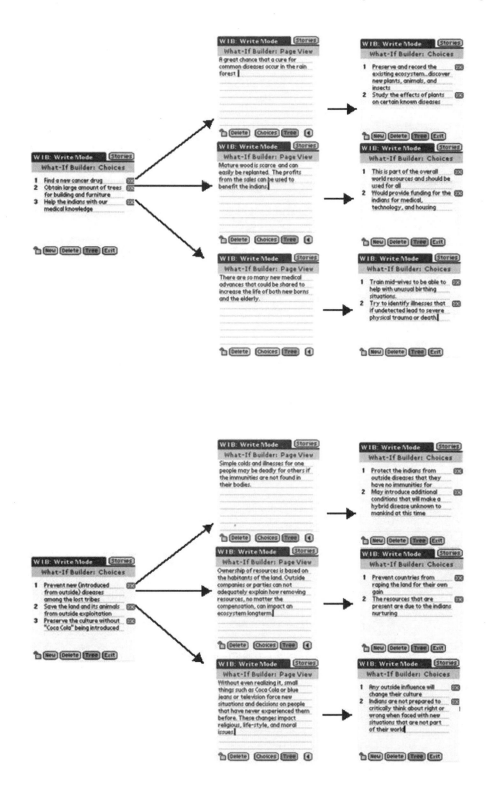

Use the Tree button to allow students to see the overall flow of the Decision Tree.

By scanning through the Decision Tree, the student reviews the options for each level.

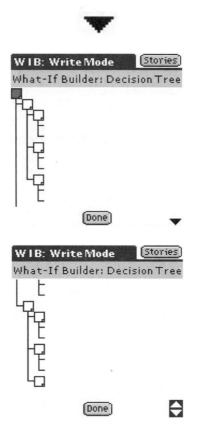

To view a page from the Decision Tree, tap on the specific option, and the Page View for that option will appear.

Defending Positions

Once the choices for the story have been established, beam the story to other students by selecting Beam Story from submenu.

Story	Edit Options Help
Delete Story... ✓D	ory List
Attach Note ✓A	
Delete Note... ✓O	Unfiled GO
Beam Story ✓B	

New   Details

Students should review the Decision Tree and select a side to defend.

Students add new options or refute existing options by using the New button at the bottom of the screen. This is an excellent opportunity to add examples or situations based on known situations in defense of positions.

After adequate time for preparation, students should present their sides in a classroom discussion or formal debate.

WIB: Write Mode   Stories

What-If Builder: Choices

1 Find a new cancer drug   GO
2 Obtain large amount of trees   GO
   for building and furniture
3 Help the indians with our   GO
   medical knowledge

New   Delete   Tree   Exit

WIB: Write Mode   Stories

What-If Builder: Page View

A great chance that a cure for common diseases occur in the rain forest |

Delete   Choices   Tree   ◀

WIB: Write Mode   Stories

What-If Builder: Choices

1 Preserve and record the   GO
   existing ecosystem...discover
   new plants, animals, and
   insects
2 Study the effects of plants   GO
   on certain known diseases

New   Delete   Tree   Exit

```
┌─────────────────────────────────────────┐
│ WIB: WriteMode        [Stories]          │
│ What-If Builder: Choices                 │
│                                          │
│ 1  Prevent new (introduced        [GO]   │
│    from outside) diseases                │
│    among the lost tribes                 │
│ 2  Save the land and its animals  [GO]   │
│    from outside exploitation             │
│ 3  Preserve the culture without   [GO]   │
│    "Coca Cola" being introduced          │
└─────────────────────────────────────────┘
        [New] [Delete] [Tree] [Exit]
```

```
┌──────────────────────────────┐      ┌──────────────────────────────┐
│ WIB: WriteMode    [Stories]   │      │ WIB: WriteMode    [Stories]   │
│ What-If Builder: Page View    │      │ What-If Builder: Choices      │
│ Simple colds and illnesses for one   │      │ 1  Protect the indians from    [GO]  │
│ people may be deadly for others if   │      │    outside diseases that they         │
│ the immunities are not found in      │      │    have no immunities for             │
│ their bodies.                        │      │ 2  May introduce additional    [GO]  │
│                                      │      │    conditions that will make a        │
│                                      │      │    hybrid disease unknown to          │
│                                      │      │    mankind at this time               │
└──────────────────────────────┘      └──────────────────────────────┘
   [Delete] [Choices] [Tree] [◄]           [New] [Delete] [Tree] [Exit]
```

3. CONTINUOUS WATER CYCLE

Overview and Learning Outcomes

Concept mapping is far more than the listing of ideas, which is an attempt to create intentionally random input in a linear fashion. Concept mapping provides an opportunity for students to generate ideas, fit ideas together, and design and communicate complex ideas, often linked to one another from a central issue or concept. Concept maps aid learning by integrating new and old knowledge explicitly; they also assess understanding and diagnose misconceptions. Although concept maps can be used across the curriculum, the map that you will develop in this activity relates the key role that energy (or lack of it) provides in a continuous water cycle.

Suggested Software Application

Palm OS: PiCoMap by GoKnow, Inc. (http://goknow.org/Products/PiCoMap.html)

Pocket PC: PiCoMap by GoKnow, Inc. (http://goknow.org/Products/PiCoMap.html) available soon

---

Grade Levels

This activity is appropriate for grade levels 2–12.

Standards

National Academies of Science

The following standards are from the National Academies of Science (1996) and can be found online at www.nap.edu/readingroom/books/nses/html/6d.html#csc58

- Science as Inquiry: Scientists formulate and test explanations of nature using observation, experiments, and theoretical and mathematical models
- Understanding About Scientific Inquiry: Technology used to gather data enhances accuracy and allows scientists to analyze and quantify results of investigations
- Life Science: Organisms and environments
- Life Science: Populations and ecosystems
- Life Science: Matter, energy, and organization in living systems
- Science in Personal and Social Perspectives: Populations, resources, and environments

International Society for Technology in Education

The following standards are from the International Society for Technology in Education (2000) and can be found online at http://cnets.iste.org/students/s_stands.html

- Basic operations and concepts: Students are proficient in the use of technology.
- Technology research tools: Students use technology to locate, evaluate, and collect information from a variety of sources.
- Technology problem-solving and decision-making tools: Students employ technology in the development of strategies for solving problems in the real world.

Calculating Your Use of Resources

Select PiCoMap from the Launcher or Home.

Select New. Enter a title and your name and tap on OK.

After studying the factors possibly contributing to the Earth's water cycle, prepare to place an initial concept on your map by drawing a circle. Immediately after releasing your stylus, a bubble (node) will appear on the screen. Enter the concept title in the bubble and tap OK at the top of the screen or anywhere else on the screen.

Continue to add bubbles for other contributing factors to the water cycle. To relocate bubbles, tap and drag them to another desired location on the screen.

Connecting Concepts

How do these factors relate to one another? How are they connected to the central concept? An edge is an element found in PiCoMap that connects two bubbles in a specific direction. Select two concepts that are interconnected. Drag your stylus from the center of one of the bubbles to the center of the other in the direction of the desired connection.

To edit a connection between concepts, tap on the edge and edit accordingly.

To change direction for a connection, tap on the edge and select Delete from the top of the screen. Drag again from the center of one bubble to the other in the direction of the desired connection.

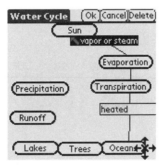

Continue to add connections between bubbles. Note that one concept may be connected to several other bubbles.

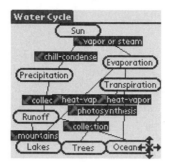

Sharing Your Map

How complete was your concept map of the water cycle? Select Beam Map from the Map menu to exchange your concept map with a partner.

Use a word processing program on your handheld computer (Quickword™ or PocketWord™) to further explain the relationships between each of the concepts on your map. Develop your own definitions for evaporation, transpiration, precipitation, and other concepts.

Individual Learning and Assessment

7

T he term "assessment" refers to activities undertaken by teachers and by their students that provide feedback to modify teaching and learning activities. Formative assessment happens when the evidence is used in a timely manner to adapt teaching to meet student needs. A handheld computer with its wireless beaming capability easily provides opportunities for formative assessment. Research has shown that networked handheld wireless devices hold great potential for improving formative assessment in a remarkably wide range of educational settings (Abrahamson, 2000).

A handheld computer, as a personal device, easily becomes an extension of the student. Students readily reach for the small computers to record personal thoughts and prove or disprove beliefs in a debate, which is precisely why this device is perfect for promoting student reflection. Whether in an analysis of how to change a student's habit of using world resources or assessing the level of achievement on a group project or the journaling on a concept, the handheld computer provides a special chronicle for a student's views.

1. IMPACTING THE WORLD'S RESOURCES

Overview and Learning Outcomes

Students calculate their personal use of the Earth's resources to maintain and improve their existence by using an Ecological Footprint Calculator. This tool measures their use of nature by calculating how much land is required to produce all the resources they consume and absorb all the waste they produce. The Ecological Footprint Calculator visualizes their "footprint" in various ways (e.g., how many Earths we would need if everyone had an identical footprint). The Earth does not have infinite resources; increasing human consumption places severe stress on the natural processes that renew some resources while depleting those resources that cannot be renewed. By using this calculator and investigating their resource use, students can design a plan of action to decrease their ecological footprint.

Suggested Software Application

EFC

Palm OS: Ecological Footprint calculator by KidSolve™, Inc. (original desktop version developed at The Concord Consortium) (www.kidsolve .com/products/palm/efc/index.html)
 Pocket PC: Available soon

Grade Levels

This activity is appropriate for grade levels 5–12.

Standards

National Academies of Science

The following standards are from the National Academies of Science (1996) and can be found online at www.nap.edu/readingroom/books/nses/html/6d.html#csc58

- Science as Inquiry: Scientists formulate and test explanations of nature using observation, experiments, and theoretical and mathematical models
- Understanding About Scientific Inquiry: Technology used to gather data enhances accuracy and allows scientists to analyze and quantify results of investigations
- Life Science: Organisms and environments
- Life Science: Populations and ecosystems
- Life Science: Matter, energy, and organization in living systems
- Science in Personal and Social Perspectives: Populations, resources, and environments
- Science in Personal and Social Perspectives: Science and technology in local, national, and global changes

- Science as Inquiry: Scientists are influenced by societal, cultural, and personal beliefs and ways of viewing the world

International Society for Technology in Education

The following standards are from the International Society for Technology in Education (2000) and can be found online at http://cnets.iste.org/students/ s_stands.html

- Basic operations and concepts: Students are proficient in the use of technology.
- Technology research tools: Students use technology to locate, evaluate, and collect information from a variety of sources.
- Technology problem-solving and decision-making tools: Students employ technology in the development of strategies for solving problems in the real world.

Calculating Your Use of Resources

Select EFC from the Launcher or Home.

Tap on + at the bottom of the screen. Add your name and date to the line and tap on GO.

Answer each of the questions by selecting the box next to your resource use.

Tap on the information button at the top of each page to further understand each question.

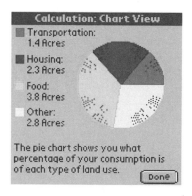

Once all the questions are answered, the screen will return to the first question. You can review your answers before displaying the graphical presentation of your use of resources.

Graphically Displaying Your Use

Display the Chart View of your ecological footprint by tapping on the pie chart at the bottom of the main screen. What type of activity used up the most acreage of land? Consider ways to decrease your use. Tap on the Done button to return to the questions.

Access the Earth View of your ecological footprint by tapping on the Earth at the bottom of the screen. How many Earths would we need if everybody consumed as much land as you do? You might even want to check out the world population by accessing the world clock at www.census.gov/main/www/popclock.html to see the total world population. Tap on the Done button to return to the questions.

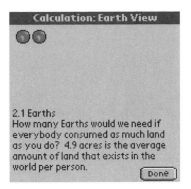

Tap on the field at the bottom of the screen to see the Field View of your ecological footprint. How many football fields represent the amount of land you consume? Tap on the Done button to return to the questions.

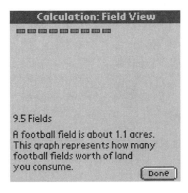

Access the Graph View of your ecological footprint by tapping on the bar graph at the bottom of the main screen when you finish your questions. How does your ecological footprint compare with the average footprint of people in other parts of the world? Tap on the Done button to return to the questions.

Proposing a Plan

Tap on the notepad at the bottom of the main screen to return to the original menu.

Highlight your name and date. Tap on EFC at the top of the screen. Select Attach Note from the Survey menu to propose a plan to decrease your ecological footprint. Share and discuss by beaming your survey with other students.

Consider your mode of transportation, your consumption of nongrazing meals, and the type of housing you use to determine a conservative plan that would impact your ecological footprint. Discuss your plans with other students.

Decreasing Your Ecological Footprint

Act on your plan by recording the following for a month, using Palm OS: QuickSheet or Pocket PC: Pocket Excel. Try to conserve on the resources.

Transportation Information

For each category of transportation, collect data for each person living with you. Then compute the total for everyone in the house and report this information below. If your data are for daily use, multiply by 30 for a monthly total. If your data are for a week, multiply by four.

- Bus mileage to and from school (miles)
- Car mileage for family events, rides with friends, etc. (miles)
- Gasoline utilized: Use the car mileage and the number of miles/gallon to determine the number of gallons your cars use

- Determine the parts to repair a car in your family: Measure the approximate weight in pounds for the repair parts
- Airplane estimation in hours traveled: Determine the hours traveled in a year and divide by 12 for a monthly average

Food Information

List food items and monthly totals.

- Vegetables, potatoes, and fruit (pounds)
- Bread (pounds)
- Rice, cereal, noodles, and other starches (pounds)
- Beans (pounds)
- Milk and yogurt (quarts)
- Cheese and butter (pounds)
- Eggs (number)
- Pork (pounds)
- Chicken and turkey (pounds)
- Beef (pounds)
- Fish (pounds)
- Juice (quarts)
- Sugar (pounds)
- Vegetable oil and fat (pounds)
- Tea and coffee (pounds)
- Garden square footage at your house that is used for food
- Eating out (number of meals)

Housing Information

- Square footage for your brick or wooden house
- Square footage of garden space that is used for nonfood plants
- Electricity (kilowatts used)
- Natural gas (cubic feet)
- Oil (gallons or pounds)
- Water usage (gallons)
- Pounds of straw used (if applicable)
- Pounds of firewood used (if applicable, even if it is just in the winter for entertainment)
- Approximate pounds of wood, if any construction has occurred in the home

Reevaluate your ecological footprint after 1 month. How did your percentages change? Did your overall use of resources change? How did you compare to other countries in the world after 1 month?

2. TEAM CHECKLIST

Overview and Learning Outcomes

Successful cooperative learning requires that each team member actively participates in the learning. Using a checklist provides the capability of assessing team member involvement in all the vital duties and member roles. Students can identify the amount and quality of completed work by individual team members and assist in the successful completion of project work.

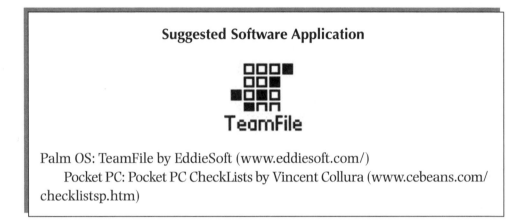

Suggested Software Application

TeamFile

Palm OS: TeamFile by EddieSoft (www.eddiesoft.com/)

Pocket PC: Pocket PC CheckLists by Vincent Collura (www.cebeans.com/checklistsp.htm)

Grade Levels

This activity is appropriate for grade levels 5–12.

Standards

National Center for History in the Schools

The following standards are from the National Center for History in the Schools (1996) and can be found online at http://www.sscnet.ucla.edu/nchs/standards

- Chronological Thinking: Compare alternative models for periodization by identifying the organizing principles on which each is based.
- Historical Comprehension: Appreciate historical perspectives—(a) describing the past on its own terms, through the eyes and experiences of those who were there, as revealed through their literature, diaries, letters, debates, arts, artifacts, and the like; (b) considering the historical context in which the event unfolded—the values, outlook, options, and contingencies of that time and place; and (c) avoiding

"present-mindedness," judging the past solely in terms of present-day norms and values.

- Historical Analysis and Interpretation: Consider multiple perspectives of various peoples in the past by demonstrating their differing motives, beliefs, interests, hopes, and fears.
- Historical Research Capabilities: Obtain historical data from a variety of sources, including library and museum collections, historic sites, historical photos, journals, diaries, eyewitness accounts, newspapers, and the like; documentary films, oral testimony from living witnesses, censuses, tax records, city directories, statistical compilations, and economic indicators.
- Historical Issues Analysis and Decision Making: Identify issues and problems in the past and analyze the interests, values, perspectives, and points of view of those involved in the situation.

National Council for the Social Studies

The following standards are from the National Council for the Social Studies (1994) and are available online at www.ncss.org/standards/toc.html/

- Time, Continuity and Change: Experiences that provide for the study of the ways human beings view themselves in and over time
- People, Places and Environments: Experiences that provide for the study of people, places, and environments

International Society for Technology in Education

The following standards are from the International Society for Technology in Education (2000) and can be found online at http://cnets.iste.org/students/ s_stands.html

- Basic operations and concepts: Students are proficient in the use of technology.
- Technology productivity tools: Students use technology tools to enhance learning, increase productivity, and promote creativity.
- Technology productivity tools: Students use productivity tools to collaborate in constructing technology-enhanced models, prepare publications, and produce other creative works.

Establishing the Teams

Select TeamFile from the Launcher or Home.

Prepare a list of projects that each team will complete. In this case, the projects relate to a study of the American Revolution.

TeamFile ▦

Select Team for checklists.

☐ Declaration of Independence
☐ Bill of Rights
☐ Boston Tea Party
■ British Invasion|
☐
☐
☐
☐

(OK)   ▲ ▼   Page 1 / 1

Tap on the box preceding each project and tap on the OK button at the bottom of the screen to add the team members.

Enter the student names on the Checklist page for the project.

Checklist ▤   List 1 / 1   ▶

Σ	Yes	No	?	▦
Jason	☐	☐	☐	--
Suzy	☐	☐	☐	--
George	☐	☐	☐	--
Mary	☐	☐	☐	--
Thomas	☐	☐	☐	--
Eric	☐	☐	☐	--
Frederico	☐	☐	☐	--
Samuel	☐	☐	☐	--

(OK)   ▲ ▼ ▯ ✎   Page 1 / 1

Repeat the process of adding names to groups by returning to the TeamFile page by tapping on the OK button and selecting each project.

Use the arrows at the bottom right of the screen to put more than 8 students on the list. A total of 48 students can be included on one project checklist.

Establishing the Tasks

Select a project from the TeamFile page and tap on the OK button.

Add the task to the top of the Checklist page.

```
Checklist 📑   List 1 / 1        ▶
Works well with others
 ε                    Yes  No  ?  🔳
   Jason               □   □   □  --
   Suzy                □   □   □  --
   George              □   □   □  --
   Mary                □   □   □  --
   Thomas              □   □   □  --
   Eric                □   □   □  --
   Frederico           □   □   □  --
   Samuel              □   □   □  --
 ( OK )   ▲  ▼  🗋 ✎  Page 1 / 1
```

Use the forward arrow at the top left of the page to add another task.

Continue to add tasks for the student project team on the header of each new Checklist page. The complete number of tasks will be displayed in the upper right corner of the screen.

```
Checklist 📑   List 8 / 8    ◀ ▶
Fluid presentation
 ε                    Yes  No  ?  🔳
   Jason               □   □   □  --
   Suzy                □   □   □  --
   George              □   □   □  --
   Mary                □   □   □  --
   Thomas              □   □   □  --
   Eric                □   □   □  --
   Frederico           □   □   □  --
   Samuel              □   □   □  --
 ( OK )   ▲  ▼  🗋 ✎  Page 1 / 6
```

Tap on the Index in the upper left corner of the screen to view the Checklist Index page.

```
        📑

Checklist Index      Page 01 / 01

Works well with others
Creates ten referenced bibliography
Listens to others
Suggests ideas
Discusses findings
Makes careful and detailed notes
Well written report
Presented well


( Go To List )   ▲  ▼   ( Cancel )
```

Return to the Checklist page by tapping on the Go To List button.

(Go To List)

Assessing Student Progress

Starting with the first task, check the boxes for the achievement to that point for each student.

Checklist 目 List 1/8 ◀ ▶	Yes	No	?	⊞
Works well with others				
Jason	☑	☐	☐	--
Suzy	☐	☑	☐	--
George	☐	☐	☑	--
Mary	☐	☑	☐	--
Thomas	☑	☐	☐	--
Eric	☑	☐	☐	--
Frederico	☑	☐	☐	--
Samuel	☑	☐	☐	--

(OK) ▲ ▼ ◻ ✎ Page 1/6

Attach a note about specific team member progress at any time by selecting the Note icon at the bottom of the screen after highlighting the prospective member.

◻

Checklist 目 List 1/8 ◀ ▶	Yes	No	?	⊞
Works well with others				
Jason	☑	☐	☐	--
Suzy	☐	☑	☐	--

Member Note

Works well with others. Initiates discussion on his own|

(OK) (Cancel) (Delete)

Tap the OK button when finished.

Checklist 目	List 8 / 8	◀ ▶			
Fluid presentation					
☎		Yes	No	?	田
Jason		☑	☐	☐	--
Suzy		☐	☑	☐	--
☐George		☑	☐	☐	--
Mary		☑	☐	☐	--
Thomas		☑	☐	☐	--
Eric		☑	☐	☐	--
Frederico		☐	☑	☐	--
Samuel		☐	☑	☐	--
(OK)	▲ ▼ ☐ ✎	Page 1 / 6			

Repeat the task analysis for each checklist.

Review the daily progress of each team by tapping on the Summation icon.

The summation will display the number of students that have completed (05), not completed (02), or are currently working on (01) the project that is in progress.

Checklist 目	List 1 / 8	◀ ▶			
Works well with others					
☎	08	05	02	01	00
Jason		☑	☐	☐	--
Suzy		☐	☑	☐	--
☐George		☐	☐	☑	--
Mary		☐	☑	☐	--
Thomas		☑	☐	☐	--
Eric		☑	☐	☐	--
Frederico		☑	☐	☐	--
Samuel		☑	☐	☐	--
(OK)	▲ ▼ ☐ ✎	Page 1 / 6			

Identifying the members of each team who have completed the task enables the progress of the team to be coordinated and monitored better.

3. CONCEPT JOURNALING

Overview and Learning Outcomes

Concept journaling makes it possible for a teacher to acquire insight into the steps, analysis, and modeling of the thoughts of each student as students work through a specific content area. By recording in a journal, students can store and search by topic and date each development. As students journal their progress of discovery, the teacher is aware of the revisions of models and can promote a continuing process of development.

Suggested Software Application

Journal

Palm OS: MicroJournal by BlackBoard Software (www.blackboardsoft ware.com)

Pocket PC: eJournal by iCE Software (http://icesoft.iwarp.com/ eJournal.htm)

Grade Levels

This activity is appropriate for grade levels 5–12.

Standards

National Academies of Science

The following standards are from the National Academies of Science (1996) and can be found online at www.nap.edu/readingroom/books/nses/ html/6d.html#csc58

- Science as Inquiry: Scientists formulate and test explanations of nature using observation, experiments, and theoretical and mathematical models
- Understanding About Scientific Inquiry: Technology used to gather data enhances accuracy and allows scientists to analyze and quantify results of investigations
- Earth and Space Science: Structure of the Earth system
- Earth and Space Science: Energy in the Earth system
- Science and Technology: Identify a problem or design an opportunity
- Science and Technology: Communicate the problem, process, and solution.

National Council of Teachers of English

The following standards are from the National Council of Teachers of English (1998) and are available online at www.readwritethink.org/standards/

- Students apply a wide range of strategies to comprehend, interpret, evaluate, and appreciate texts. They draw on their prior experience, their interactions with other readers and writers, their knowledge of word meaning and of other texts, their word identification strategies, and their understanding of textual features (e.g., sound-letter correspondence, sentence structure, context, graphics).
- Students use a variety of technological and information resources (e.g., libraries, databases, computer networks, video) to gather and synthesize information and to create and communicate knowledge.

International Society for Technology in Education

The following standards are from the International Society for Technology in Education (2000) and can be found online at http://cnets.iste.org/students/ s_stands.html

- Basic operations and concepts: Students are proficient in the use of technology.
- Technology research tools: Students use technology tools to enhance learning, increase productivity, and promote creativity.
- Technology problem-solving and decision-making tools: Students employ technology in the development of strategies for solving problems in the real world.

Formulating a Journal Entry

Select the Journal icon from the Launcher or Home.

Tap on the Date line and select, from the calendar, the month and date that you are journaling. If the date is the same as the day you are recording the journal, tap on the Today button.

The following is one suggestion for the journaling of a concept. In this case, the subject is meteorology. Regardless of the specific subject, it is important that the reflection follows a structure. Although stream of consciousness, another way of recording thoughts, is a very free and comfortable style of reflection, it is not effective for organizing a plan of research. Start by recalling the pertinent facts about the lesson. What were the important points?

MicroJournal 2.1

Date   9/8/03

Subject   What is weather?

Major thoughts from the class:
• Changes in weather are caused by movements of large air masses
• When two air masses with different properties meet, a boundary called a

[Next] [First] [Add] [List]
[Prev] [Last] [Del] [Beam]

Think carefully about how this particular lesson affects you or relates personally to you. How does this apply to your daily life? Do you have any insights or examples of situations that have occurred locally, nationally, or globally?

MicroJournal 2.1

Date   9/8/03

Subject   What is weather?

How does this affect me?
Every morning I watch the weather man on tv. When he talks about a movement of high or low pressure of air into my area, I now know that the

[Next] [First] [Add] [List]
[Prev] [Last] [Del] [Beam]

Often, after hearing new information, questions will arise in your mind after you have thought about situations that have impacted you. List any questions that you would like answered after the lesson.

MicroJournal 2.1

Date   9/8/03

Subject   What is weather?

Questions that I have are:
• What causes a high and low area of pressure?
• What is the affect of a high and low pressure area meeting?

[Next] [First] [Add] [List]
[Prev] [Last] [Del] [Beam]

Depending on the lesson, develop a plan of action or investigation that will aid in understanding the concept. Propose a challenge that will answer previously stated questions.

Beam or synch your log to the teacher. This will make it possible for your proposed questions, as well as your suggested methods of investigation or challenges, to be approved by a teacher.

$$\boxed{\text{Beam}}$$

Daily Logging

Continue to log daily in the journal. Add to the format any outcomes from the answers to the questions and the challenges or investigations.

Review any past logs by tapping on the List icon at the bottom of the screen and selecting a specific log.

$$\boxed{\text{List}}$$

Journaling can be a powerful tool to reflect systematically on your experiences, observations, feelings, and depth of understanding. Additions to the journal can include reviews of texts, articles, simulations, or Web sites in addition to comments and notes on the daily classroom lesson.

Empowering Teachers

8

At the center of effective use of instructional technology is the teacher. The pedagogical climate changes when the environment changes from teacher centered to student centered, and the teacher's role is critical in enabling this shift. Teachers must be able to make wise, informed decisions about technology in order for students to become comfortable and effective users of various technologies (Office of Technology Assessment, 1995). School leaders also play an important role in the successful integration of handheld computers. Too many times, technology is purchased for schools only to sit on the shelf, seldom, if ever, used by teachers or students. This is not due to lack of good intentions or inherent limitations of the technology; rather, it reflects the school's failure to work effectively as a cohesive educational community through the many stages of technology implementation and integration. By asking and answering the following questions, those curricular and technology teachers who are interested in handheld computer adoption will vastly improve the chances of success.

Will the use of handheld computers support our goals for our students?

The answer to this question is not as easy as it seems. Teachers must be confident in applying the technology in appropriate situations to meet their students' needs. Inventory the computing needs of your school district by dialoguing with other teachers, school board members, students, and parents. Polling, surveying, or interviewing the community will likely expose a multitude of concerns, ranging from equity issues to effective use of existing technology. Provide a forum for public discussion around the areas that need improvement by sponsoring open public meetings, with invited technology researchers and experts as speakers (Staudt, 2002b). After listening carefully to public and internal response, select an advisory group that consists of vocal and committed teachers, administrators, parents, and students. Their mission is to prioritize the list of concerns and to identify the specific needs that will be aided by the use of handheld computers (Pownell & Bailey, 2000). If the decision of the advisory team is to proceed with the implementation of handheld computers in the schools, the advisory team will need to research the different handheld solutions and their ability to meet your needs. To research the technical capabilities, consult Usight (http://usight.concord.org/suppliers).

How does use of these tools support and change classroom teaching?

Although the learning curve for students using handhelds is very rapid, teachers must be comfortable and familiar with the tools. The ease with which teachers can use and integrate new technologies in support of curricular and assessment goals is at the heart of two important goals for beneficial technology integration: using technology to support learning rather than as an add-on, and moving to more student-directed and collaborative learning while maintaining classroom management. Issues around the latter goal may be resolved by honoring the teaching pedagogies of individual teachers while the transition to handheld technology is managed. Teaching methods vary from one teacher to another and among grade levels. Teachers can locate their own readiness level and entry point by looking at their own teaching styles and asking the following questions:

- Are my classroom methods teacher centered or student centered?
- Do I promote active learning techniques and require student collaboration?
- Do I provide freedom for students to explore?
- Do I encourage opportunities for the students to ask questions, research solutions, and resolve conflicts?

Teachers who do not encourage or adopt these techniques should not be expected to embrace both a new technology and a drastic change in teaching style at the same time. Pervasive computing that is available at all times and places may be an intrusion in a teacher-centered classroom. Handheld computers by nature are highly personal, portable tools that promote the flow of information and communication. This flow of information and communication can also mean a change of culture, one for which the teacher must be prepared.

Start small and build a strong foundation for systemic implementation with a small volunteer pilot group of teachers. Based on their inquiry-based methods, communication skills, and mentoring abilities, choose a team of teachers who will pilot the use of handheld computers in the classroom. Teachers can meet with the advisory team to obtain information about the production, collaboration, and research tools that can be accessed while using the technology. All teachers in the pilot group should commit to experimenting, testing varying methods, and assessing progress throughout the year. The advisory team, pilot teachers, and administration can design a plan for obtaining and distributing the handheld computers.

Implementing the plan will mean providing ample time and money for professional development. Making decisions about the specifics of how that time and money will be spent needs to include attention to the following:

- Building comfort
- Articulating connections between technology use and curricular goals
- Establishing methods of assessing learning

A tried-and-true method of teacher professional development is one that stresses

- The pedagogy
- Familiarity with the tool
- Improvement of classroom content understanding
- Testing activities to be used with students in the form of a practicum (Technology Enhanced Elementary and Middle School Science, 2002, and *International Netcourse Teacher Enhancement Coalition*, 1998)

A practicum is designed by the teacher and reviewed by other pilot teachers before use in the classroom. Supplementing face-to-face workshops with online courses provides a strong structure for success. Online help can provide a safety net that speeds teachers' surmounting of obstacles. This type of professional development requires ongoing moderation and additional preparation and collaboration by teachers throughout the school year. This initial investment pays ultimate dividends in the forms of a strengthened learning community, stronger teaching, and learning experiences for students that are more consonant with real life.

As mentioned earlier, handheld computers are personal tools, and because these personal tools are placed in the hands of students, issues of student use—including appropriate behavior, ethics, and accountability—must be addressed and fully discussed with students and parents. Without established protocols and techniques that define and teach responsible use, presence of these tools can be challenging to classroom management. Teachers should share methods by discussing options around such questions as the following:

- To what extent should the classroom be paperless?
- Should every student have a handheld?

- How do we best share student data?
- Should the computers go home with the students at night?
- How do we assess student progress?

Use of online forums provides excellent avenues for this type of discourse.

Will the use of handheld computers help meet student needs?

Schools have spent a great deal of time designing course goals and objectives that are aligned to existing national or state standards. It is imperative that student use extends beyond the traditional organizational use of a handheld computer to a student inquiry and collaboration approach, which promotes the flow of information and communication into the existing curriculum. National content standards and many state standards in mathematics, science, and social studies include requirements for students to become proficient at analyzing and displaying data in multiple ways and at communicating about content, research, and problem solving. In addition, many of the National Educational Technology Standards will be realized by the use of better productivity, communication, research, data collection, and problem-solving tools available on handheld computers (International Society for Technology in Education, 2000). To review existing educational cross-curricula software applications, correlation to standards, and project starters that are suggested by teachers using handheld computers in their classrooms, consult Palm Applications in Education (http://pie.concord.org).

Is there a successful support system in place for the systemic use of handheld computers?

Providing resources and support for teachers is imperative for successful implementation. Technology personnel must be knowledgeable about handheld software, plus hardware add-ons such as cameras, sensors, global positioning systems, adapters, and cables. Supporting instructional materials should be available to teachers as well. Integrating technical support, both onsite and online, into the overall professional development plan keeps technology personnel informed of all problems and difficulties in transferring software and data. Technical support personnel who are experienced in education will also become assets in promoting self-sufficiency on the part of the pilot teachers by modeling relevant problem-solving skills. Because handheld computers are constantly improving in memory and features, additional updates in hardware and applications will be required on a regular basis. Often, students are excellent supplements to the pool of technology expertise in the classroom and school.

How can we ensure ongoing evaluations of effectiveness?

Open communication and assessment of progress with the entire educational community will ensure continuation of the implementation beyond the pilot group. Regular feedback from the pilot teachers, both in written evaluations and in public presentations, will assist in achieving this goal. If handheld computers are used for educational pursuits beyond mere planning or organizing (the model for use in the business world), students will demonstrate their ubiquity in locations inside and outside the school. Providing samples of student work and curriculum integration in school newsletters will promote discussion on the part of future users—by parents, teachers, and students.

After the first year, the pilot teachers, initial student users, moderators, and technical support personnel should be involved in the next wave of professional development. Experienced users should design and participate in future face-to-face professional development and online discussion forums to build an ongoing support network. As with any educational innovation, expansion will depend on the school's overall commitment to the full integration of handhelds, the willingness of the teachers to participate, and the availability of hardware, software, and continuing support.

What future trends might we expect?

Over the next decade, handheld computers will change a great deal, so it is unreasonable to use the current models as a guide. Central processing unit (CPU) power will increase by a factor of 100, as will networking bandwidth and memory capacity (Tinker, 2000). This rapidly changing technology promises many additional improvements and advances, such as embedded assessments, increased storage and sorting capabilities, improved networking, and design changes so students can wear these small computers.

Recently developed curriculum residing on handheld computers explores the use of embedded assessments. The Technology Enhanced Elementary and Middle School Science project placed entire science investigations on handheld computers, linking and automatically storing student responses to embedded questions (Technology Enhanced Elementary and Middle School Science, 2002). The student input is easily time-stamped by individual handheld computers and beamed to teachers and students for instantaneous review of student understanding and the identification of misconceptions. As a result of this research, many additional applications by companies are being created to enhance formative, as well as summative, assessments.

Prev | Next | ▼ Introduction | Done

TEEMSS

Heat Flow Introduction

Discovery Question:

What happens when two objects at different temperatures are left in contact with each other?

Prev | Next | ▼ Trial I | Done

tip·········

3. What will happen when you touch the end of the probe and then let go? What happens when you put the probe in water?

Question 1. predict water

Name Question 1. predict wate | Done

1.1 What will happen when you touch the end of the probe and then let go?

The temperature will first increase and then rapidly decrease.

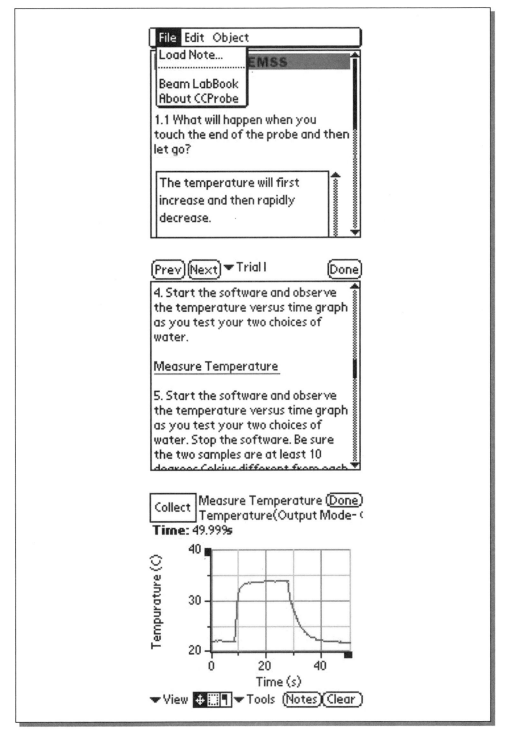

Additional research through the Modeling Across the Curriculum project (http://mac.concord.org/) is testing embedded guidance and assessment for students in specialized online activities. A specialized software environment called Pedagogica communicates and controls each computer activity based on a student's response or action. A learner's interactions with the software are controlled through Pedagogica by changing the available options, the nature of the scaffolding (or guidance tools), instructions, and the assessments viewed by each individual student. All interactions and paths that the student chooses or that are automatically selected are stored and reported to the teacher. This software is currently available for desktop computers, and plans are in place to provide a similar environment for handheld computers (Modeling Across the Curriculum, 2001).

Secure digital (SD) cards are thumbnail-size removal storage devices that can contain textbooks, encyclopedias, and many other reference materials. They fit into slots on handheld computers, making it possible to search a vast amount of information easily. Their use also combines the abilities of students to predict, highlight, take notes, and respond to questions directly on the reference source—truly making the educational medium rich, relevant, and interactive!

According to Nick Micozzi (2003), a typical high school science textbook costs around $60.00. Generally, these textbooks are not updated for at least 5–8 years. Companies such as Beyond Books (www.beyondbooks.com/) provide, on an SD card, up-to-date materials in science, literature, language arts, and social studies for around $1.00 per student per year. Coupling this with EBSCO's online journals (http://ejournals.ebsco.com/) accessible through the Web using handheld computers equipped with wireless connections (around $1.20 per student) results in savings per student per year of $5.55 over use of traditional textbooks. For a student body of 1,500 students, this savings adds up to more than $40,000 in 5 years. This money could be used to purchase about 400 handheld computers in today's market (Micozzi, 2003).

Affordable wireless networking capabilities are rapidly becoming a reality on handheld computers. The Data and Models project (2001; refer to www.concord.org/data-models/) studied how a student's mental models agreed with his or her observations, such as when a phenomenon observed in one situation fails to repeat itself on a larger scale. Handheld computers equipped with 32 MB of memory, a color screen, and 802.11b wireless Ethernet capability were used to support student explorations of various forms of heat energy transfer. The students explored thermal conductivity in a set of small aluminum, stainless steel, and nylon blocks with an embedded (wireless) network of temperature sensors. Small transmitting wireless sensors, like these temperature sensors, are rapidly coming into use in many medical and other monitoring situations. The blocks can be arranged in arbitrary two-dimensional patterns, and heat can be pumped either into or out of any point of the thermal network of blocks using a Peltier-based thermal actuator. The temperature readings of sensors embedded in the blocks are transmitted over a wireless Ethernet and displayed simultaneously on multiple handheld computers (Bannasch, 2001).

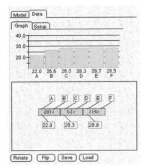

The students adjust theories by confronting their mental models with evidence consisting of real-time data. For example, in one study (Staudt & Horwitz, 2001), students during testing made the statement that "heat cannot move around corners." After heating the metal blocks embedded with temperature probes in different configurations, the students quickly realized that heat can travel through metal, no matter what the alignment of the bars. Yet they still held to some of their original theories: Although heat moves around corners, it "moves more slowly." Later, students challenged this misconception with side-by-side setups with different metal block configurations, careful analysis of the graphs, and a stopwatch. This type of investigation would not be possible without wireless sensor and handheld capabilities.

New Bluetooth™ wireless technology embedded in some handheld computers or on Bluetooth cards provides local area networking collaboration with up to seven other students simultaneously. A short-ranged Bluetooth™ network is supported within a 30-foot radius. Using BlueBoard's or BlueChat's "collaborative white boards," the drawings or statements of one member of a group are viewed by all. Any group member can, in turn, adjust the drawing or respond to the statement instantly.

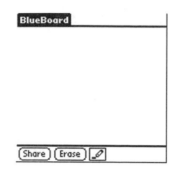

Other wireless systems are being tested in informal museum settings. The Exploratorium in San Francisco, California, is experimenting with retractable (yo-yo) and wearable (watch and necklace) systems and cards that track visitors' conceptual pathways throughout the museum as they interact with certain exhibits. This information is placed on personalized Web pages so that after the museum trip, visitors can review additional science articles, conduct personally relevant science investigations, explore online exhibits, and download hands-on kits and other science activities at home. This ID capture system has an embedded wireless transceiver RFID tag, developed by Texas Instruments and Intel Research Labs (Hsi, 2004). Imagine tracking a student's conceptual endeavors much the same way throughout the school day. Using either a handheld computer or another computing device, students could automatically mount work on their own Web page for individualized homework, parental review, and a wealth of additional activities to pique their curiosity.

In fact, the MIT Media Lab has been designing and testing wearable computing for some time. Its developers contend that a person's computer should be worn, much as eyeglasses or clothing are worn, and interact with the user based on the context of the situation. With heads-up displays employing computer screens embedded in eyeglasses, unobtrusive input devices, personal wireless local area networks, virtual keypads that project beams on tabletops, and a host of context-sending and communication tools, the wearable computer can act as an intelligent assistant. To learn more about wearable computing, visit www.media.mit.edu/wearables/

As are many technologies, handheld computers are constantly improving in features and hardware capabilities. As more teachers use these devices, developers of software applications are answering the call for additional software and functionality to meet the needs of a sophisticated educational audience.

FINAL THOUGHTS

Handheld computers enable students to engage in active, creative, and reflective investigations. I am forever amazed with how students push the limits, no matter what grade level they are in. When a pair of second-graders used a handheld computer with an attached temperature probe using an ImagiWorks™ sensor interface, they worked as a team to ask questions. They first took the temperature of the air and then investigated the shady area around a tree on the playground. They investigated the temperature down a drainage hole and both the basketball blacktop and the white line that bordered the court. After taking notes on the handheld computer and discussing the differences, the students turned to the shoes they were wearing. How different is the temperature of the air from my shoe? How does the temperature of my shoe compare to the temperature in the shade? Things that made the temperature change intrigued them. As the two stood and reviewed the readings, they compared and discussed the differences. Then they verbalized their own experimental procedure: Let's test the temperature of the air, our shoes, and our shoes while we walk. As a result, these second graders designed their own experimental procedure and analyzed the results on a very sophisticated level for the age group. Although this age group does not yet formalize the idea of friction and heat, these two young boys were well on their way to developing an understanding based on the context of their investigation.

As I hope the sample activities throughout this book have demonstrated, handheld computers offer the promise of putting affordable computers in the hands of every student in order to meet standards across subject areas—from math to English, social studies to science, and, of course, technology—and to promote inquiry-based learning, student collaboration, and communication. In a galaxy not so far away, it's time educators hear "Beam me up, Teacher!" from every student.

References

Abrahamson, L. (2000). *Equity impacts from formative assessment using a classroom communication system (CCS) in 3rd through 5th grades.* Menlo Park, CA: Center for Innovative Learning Technologies Presentations, SRI International. Abstract retrieved from http://www.cilt.org/events/2000/body_cilt2000_submissions.html

Bannasch, S. (2001). Wireless computers and probeware support a new science curriculum: Using iPAQ Pocket PCS to study science fundamentals. *The Concord Consortium, 5*(1). Retrieved from www.concord.org/newsletter/2001spring/newscience.html

Bransford, J. D., Brown, A. L., & Cocking, R. R. (Eds.). (1999). *How people learn: Brain, mind, experience, and school.* Washington, DC: National Academy Press.

Brasell, H. (1987). The effect of real-time laboratory graphing on learning representations of distance and velocity. *Journal of Research in Science Teaching, 24*(4), 385–395.

Darling-Hammond, L. (1997). School reform at the crossroads: Confronting the central issues of teaching. *Educational Policy, 11*(2), 151–166.

Data and models project. (2001). The Concord Consortium. Retrieved from www.concord.org/data-models/

DataGotchi Deep Dive. (1998). Menlo Park, CA: Center for Innovative Learning Technologies, SRI International. Retrieved from www.cilt.org/images/DataGotchi.pdf

Hsi, S. (2004, March). *I-Guides in progress: Two prototype applications for museum educators and visitors using wireless technologies to support informal science learning.* Paper presented at the 2nd IEEE International Workshop on Wireless and Mobile Technologies in Education (WMTE'04), Taiwan.

International Netcourse Teacher Enhancement Coalition. (1998). The Concord Consortium. Retrieved from http://archive.concord.org/intec/

International Society for Technology in Education. (2000). *National educational technology standards for students.* Retrieved from http://cnets.iste.org/students/s_stands.html

Micozzi, N. (2003, October). *Planning for the next generation science instructional environment.* Presentation at the National Science Teachers Association convention, Minneapolis, MN.

Modeling Across the Curriculum. (2001). Interagency Education Research Initiative (IERI) jointly supported by National Science Foundation, the U.S. Department of Education, and the National Institute of Child Health and Human Development (Grant No. REC-0115699), The Concord Consortium, Harvard University, and Northwestern University. Retrieved from http://mac.concord.org

National Academies of Science. (1966). *National Science Education Standards : Observe, interact, change, learn.* Washington, DC: National Academy Press. Retrieved from www.nap.edu/readingroom/books/nses/html/6d.html#csc58

National Center for Education Statistics. (2000). *Internet access in U.S. public schools, Fall 2000 (FRSS 79).* Washington, DC: U.S. Department of Education.

National Center for History in the Schools. (1996). *National Standards for History.* Los Angeles: Author.

National Council for the Social Studies. (1994). *Expectations of excellence: Curriculum standards for social studies.* Washington, DC. Retrieved from www.ncss.org/standards/toc.html/

National Council of Teachers of English. (1998). *IRA/NCTE standards for the English language arts.* Retrieved from www.readwritethink.org/standards/

National Council of Teachers of Mathematics. (2000). *NCTM principles & standards for school mathematics.* Retrieved from www.standards.nctm.org/document/chapter1/index.htm

National Research Council. (1999). *How people learn: Brain, mind, experience and school.* Washington, DC: National Academy Press.

Norris, C. A., & Soloway, E. M. (2003, April). The viable alternative: Handhelds. *The School Administrator.* Retrieved from www.aasa.org/publications/sa/2003_04/soloway.htm

November, A. (2001). *Empowering students with technology.* Arlington Heights, IL: SkyLight Training and Publishing.

Office of Technology Assessment, Congress of the United States. (1995). *Teachers & Technology: Making the connection.* Washington, DC: Author.

Partnership for 21st Century Skills. (2002). *Learning for the 21st century.* Retrieved from http://www.21stcenturyskills.org/downloads/P21_Report.pdf

Pownell, D., & Bailey, G. D. (2000). Handheld computing for educational leaders: A tool for organizing or empowerment. *Learning and Leading With Technology, 27*(8). Retrieved from www.educatorspalm.org/hhl/leadership/leadarticle.html

Roschelle, J., Penuel, B., & Abrahamson, L. (2003). *Using classroom networks to improve achievement and participation in mathematics and science.* Menlo Park, CA: SRI International and Better Education.

SRI International & Palm, Inc. (2002). *Palm Education Pioneers final report.* Retrieved from www.palmgrants.sri.com/findings.html

Staudt, C. (2002a). Handhelds track student progress: Instant feedback through beaming identifies student misconceptions. *The Concord Consortium, 6*(1). Retrieved from www.concord.org/newsletter/2002winter/handhelds.html

Staudt, C. (2002b). The ten commandments of technology implementation: Integrating handheld computers effectively into schools. *USight* [*The Concord Consortium*]. Retrieved from http://usight.concord.org/new/tcti.html

Staudt, C., & Horwitz, P. (2001). Reconciling conflicting evidence: Researchers use models and handhelds to investigate how students learn science. *The Concord Consortium, 5*(1). Retrieved from www.concord.org/newsletter/2001spring/evidence.html

Summerfield, L. M. (1995). *National standards for school health education.* Washington, DC: ERIC Clearinghouse on Teaching and Teacher Education. (ERIC Document Reproduction Service No. ED387483). Retrieved from www.ericfacility.net/ ericdigests/ed387483.html

Technology Enhanced Elementary and Middle School Science. (2002). Retrieved from www.concord.org/teemss

Thornton, R. (1999, January). *Using the results of research in science education to improve science learning.* Keynote address to the International Conference on Science Education, Nicosia, Cyprus.

Tinker, R. (2000). What's new. *USight, The Concord Consortium.* Retrieved from http://usight.concord.org/new/

U.S. Department of Labor, Employment & Training Administration. (1991, June). *What work requires of schools* (SCANS [The Secretary's Commission on Achieving Necessary Skills] Report for America 2000). Washington, DC: Author. Retrieved from http://wdr.doleta.gov/SCANS/whatwork/

Bibliography

Ammer, J., et al. (2000). *PicoRadio supports ad hoc ultra-low power wireless networking.* Pico Radio Group. Berkeley Wireless Research Center. [Online]. Available: http://bwrc.eecs.berkeley.edu/Background/IEEE%20Computer%20Magazine%20Article/r7042b.pdf

Bailey, G. (1996). Technology leadership: Ten essential buttons for understanding technology integration in the 21st century. *Educational Considerations, 23*(2), 2–6.

Bailey, G., & Lumley, D. (1999, January). Fishing the Net: Teach kids what to keep and what to throw back. *Electronic School, 186*(1), A20–A23. [Online]. Available: http://www.electronic-school.com/199901/0199f4.html

Bailey, G., & Lumley, D. (1997). *Staff development in technology: A sourcebook for teachers, technology leaders, and school administrators.* Bloomington, IN: National Educational Service.

Bailey, G. D., & Lumley, D. (1994). *Technology staff development programs: A leadership sourcebook for school administrators.* New York: Scholastic.

Bailey, G. D., Lumley, D., & Dunbar, D. (1995). *Leadership & technology—What school board members need to know.* Alexandria, VA: National School Boards Association.

Ballard, M. (2000, November/December). Technology lead teachers. *Multimedia Schools, 7*(6). Available: http://usight.concord.org/what/bibliography/biblio-h-p.html

Bannasch, S. (2000). Beam me up, Scottie!: Handheld computers extend the range of wireless communication in schools. *The Concord Consortium, 4*(3). [Online]. Available: http://www.concord.org/newsletter/2000fall/beam.html

Bannasch, S. (1999, Fall). The electronic curator: Using a handheld computer at the Exploratorium. *The Concord Consortium.* [Online]. Available: http://www.concord.org/newsletter/1999fall/electronic-curator.html

Beattie, R. (2000, September). The truth about tech support. *Electronic School.* [Online]. Available: http://www.electronic-school.com/2000/09/0900f3.html

Bilezikjian, M., Mandryk, R. L., Klemmer, S. R., Inkpen, K. M., & Landay, J. A. (2000, November). *Exploring a new interaction paradigm for collaborating on handheld computers.* UC Berkeley Computer Science Division Technical Report.

Broderson, R. W. (1999). Berkeley Wireless Research Center—Past, present, future. *Mobile Computing Communications Review, 3*(1).

Crawford, K., & Staudt, C. (1999, Fall). A computer in the palm of their hands. *The Concord Consortium.* [Online]. Available: http://www.concord.org/newsletter/1999fall/palm-computer.html

Crawford, V., & Vahey, P. (2002, March). *Palm Education pioneers program evaluation report*. SRI, Palm, Inc. [Online]. Available: http://palmgrants.sri.com/PEP_R2_Report.pdf

Curtis, M., & Soloway, E. (in press). *A hands-on guide to using Palm computers in K-12.*

DataGotchi Deep Dive. (1998). Menlo Park, CA: Center for Innovative Learning Technologies, SRI International [Online]. Available: http://www.cilt.org/images/DataGotchi.pdf

Davies, N., Blair, G. S., & Hutchison, D. (1999). *GUIDE: Context-sensitive mobile multimedia support for city visitors. Summary of end of award report*. Available: http://www.guide.lancs.ac.uk/GuideReportSummary.html

Decker, C., & Beigl, M. (2002). *Data paths in wearable communication networks*. International conference on Architecture of Computing Systems (ARCS). [Online]. Available: http://www.teco.edu/~michael/publication/decker_beigl_arc2002_final.pdf

Druin, A. (1999). The role of children in the design of new technology. *Behaviour and Information Technology*. [Online]. Available: ftp://ftp.cs.umd.edu/pub/hcil/Reports-Abstracts-Bibliography/99-23html/99-23.html

Frauenfelder, M. (1999, July 9). The future is at hand. *The Industry Standard.*

Fulton, K. (1998). Kathleen Fulton on evaluating the effectiveness of educational technology. *Academy for Educational Development*. [Online]. Available: http://millennium.aed.org/fulton.shtml

Grant, W. C. (1993). Wireless Coyote: A computer-supported field trip. *Communications of the ACM, 36*(5), 57–59.

Havinga, P. J. M. (2000, February). *Mobile multimedia systems*. Ph.D. thesis, University of Twente. [Online]. Available: http://wwwhome.cs.utwente.nl/~havinga/thesis/index.html

Heinecke, W. F., Blasi, L., Milman, N., & Washington, L. (1999). New directions in the evaluation of the effectiveness of educational technology. *The Secretary's Conference on Educational Technology*. [Online]. Available: http://www.ed.gov/Technology/TechConf/1999/whitepapers/paper8.html

Hsi, S. (2000). *Using handheld technologies to connect Web-based learning to outdoor investigations*. Paper presented at NARST 2000, National Association for Research in Science Teaching Annual Meeting, April 30–May 3.

Hsi, S., Collison, J., & Staudt, C. (2000). *Bridging Web-based science learning with outdoor inquiry using Palm computers*. Presentation to American Education Researcher Association Annual Meeting, New Orleans, April 24–28.

Inkpen, K. M. (1999). Designing handheld technologies for kids. *Personal Technologies Journal, 3*(1–2), 88–89. Available: http://www.cs.sfu.ca/people/Faculty/inkpen/Papers/hcscw_inkpen.pdf

International Data Corporation. (1997). *Understanding the total cost and value of integrating technology in schools*. Framingham, MA: Author.

Johnson, D., & Nissenbaum, H. (1995). *Computers, ethics, and social values*. Upper Saddle River, NJ: Prentice Hall.

Jonassen, D. H. (2000). *Computers as mind tools for schools: Engaging critical thinking* (2nd ed.). Upper Saddle River, NJ: Merrill.

Jones, M. L. W., Rieger, R. H., Treadwell, P., & Gay, G. (2000, June). Live from the stacks: User feedback on mobile computers and wireless tools for library patrons. *ACM Digital Library.* Available: http://www.nomad.cornell.edu/research/stacksrpt.htm

Kindberg, T., & Barton, J. (2001). A Web-based nomadic computing system. *Tim Computer Networks, 35,* 443–456.

Kirk, H. (2001). *Accessibility and new technology in the museum.* Paper presented at Museums and the Web 2001 Conference, Seattle, WA, March 15–17. Available: http://www.archimuse.com/mw2001/papers/kirk/kirk.html

Landay, J. A., & Davis, R. C. (1999). Making sharing pervasive: Ubiquitous computing for shared note taking. *IBM Systems Journal, 38*(4), 531–550.

Landay, J. A., Davis, R. C., Chen, V., Huang, H., Lee, R. B., Li, F., Lin, J., Morrey, C. B., III, & Schleimer, B. (1998). *NotePals: Sharing and synchronizing handwritten notes with multimedia documents.* Presented at Handheld CSCW Workshop: CSCW 98, Seattle, WA, November 14.

Linn, M. C., & Hsi, S. (2000). *Computers, teachers, peers: Science learning partners.* Mahwah, NJ: Lawrence Erlbaum Associates.

Long, S., Kooper, R., Abowd, G. D., & Atkeson, C. G. (1996, November). Rapid prototyping of mobile context-aware applications: The cyberguide case study. In *Proceedings of the 2nd ACM International Conference on Mobile Computing and Networking (MobiCom '96).*

Lorion, M., & Staudt, C. (2000). The future of handheld computers in education: A conversation with Palm, Inc. *The Concord Consortium.* [Online]. Available: http://www.concord.org/newsletter/2000fall/futureofhandhelds.html

Lumley, D., & Bailey, G. (1997). *Planning for technology: A guidebook for teachers, technology leaders, and school administrators.* Best Practices Series, National Educational Service.

Mandryk, R. L., Inkpen, K. M., Bilezikjian, M., Klemmer, S. R., & Landay, J. A. (2001, April). Supporting children's collaboration across handheld computers. In *Extended Abstracts of CHI 2001, Conference on Human Factors in Computing Systems,* Seattle, WA, pp. 255–256.

Martin, W., Rieger, R., & Gay, G. (1999). *Designing across disciplines: Negotiating collaborator interests in a digital museum project.* International Cultural Heritage Informatics Meeting, Washington, DC.

McKenzie, J. (1997). Ending the siege: Introducing technologies to the regular classroom. *From Now On.*

McNabb, M., Hawkes, M., & Rouk, U. (1999). *Critical issues in evaluating the effectiveness of technology.* The Secretary's Conference on Educational Technology.

Means, B., Blando, J., Olson, K., Middleton, T., Remz, A., & Zorfass, J. (1993). *Using technology to support education reform.* Washington, DC: U.S. Department of Education.

Moursund, D. (1998, April). Some "hidden" costs of computers. *Learning and Leading with Technology.*

Novak, T. P., & Hoffman, D. L. (1998, February 2). *Bridging the digital divide: The impact of race on computer access and Internet use.* Project 2000 Vanderbilt University. [Online]. Available: http://elab.vanderbilt.edu/research/papers/html/manuscripts/race/science.html

November, A. (2001). *Empowering students with technology.* Chicago: Skylight Professional Development.

Olsson, T. (1997). Students with eMates take to the field: Learning science by doing science. *Apple Learning Technology Review.* Available: http://www.apple.com/education/LTReview/fa1197/main2/default.html

Osuma, R. (2001, March 15). Handheld computers becoming increasingly popular. *Air Force News Archive.* [Online]. Available: http://www.af.mil/news/Mar2001/n20010315_0370.shtml

Parhan, C. (1997). The trouble with technology planning. *Technology and Learning, 18*(2), 47.

Pea, R., & Sheingold, K. (Eds.). (1987). *Mirrors of minds: Patterns of experience in educational computing.* Norwood, NJ: Ablex.

Perkins, J. (2000, September 30). *Handscape project description: An investigation of wireless technology in the museum community.* [Online]. Available: http://www.cimi.org/wg/handscape/Handscape_long_desc.html

Pownell, D., & Bailey, G. D. (2001, June). Getting a handle on handhelds. *Electronic School.* [Online]. Available: http://www.electronicschool.com/2001/06/0601handhelds.html

Pownell, D., & Bailey, G. D. (2000). Handheld computing for educational leaders: A tool for organizing or empowerment. *Learning and Leading with Technology, 27*(8), 46–49, 59–60.

Rieger, R., & Gay, G. (1997). *Using mobile computing to enhance field study.* Proceedings from the Computer-Supported Collaborative Learning Conference: CSCL 97, Toronto, December 10–14, pp. 215–223.

Ringle, M., & Updegrove, D. (1998, November 1). *Is strategic planning for technology an oxymoron?* [Online]. Available: http://www.educause.edu/ir/library/html/cem9814.html

Rosenbaum, D. (2000, August). Power structure. *Portable Computing.*

Sandholtz, J., Ringstaff, C., & Dwyer, D. (1997). *Teaching with technology: Creating student-centered classrooms.* New York: Teachers College Press.

Sawhney, N., Abowd, G., & Atkeson, C. (1996). *Georgia Institute of Technology.* [Online]. Available: http://www.cc.gatech.edu/fce/c2000/pubs/chi96/index.html

Schofield, J. W. (1995). *Computers and classroom culture.* New York: Cambridge University Press.

Schwartz, K. D. (2000). It's a tool, not a toy. *Mobile Computing & Communication, 11*(5), 77–84.

Sharples, M. (2000). The design of personal mobile technologies for lifelong learning. *Computers & Education, 34,* 177–193.

Shields, J. (2001, March). Wireless networks come of age. *Technology & Learning.*

Soloway, E., Grant, W., Tinker, R., Roschelle, J., Mills, M., Resnick, M., Berg, R., & Eisenberg, M. (1999). Science in the palm of their hands. *Communications of the ACM, 42*(8), 21–26.

Soloway, E., Norris, C., Blumenfeld, P., Fishman, B., Krajcik, J., & Marx, R. (2001, June). Devices are ready-at-hand. *Communications of the ACM.* Available: http://www.handheld.hice-dev.org/readyAtHand.htm

Spasojevic, M., & Kindberg, T. (2001). *A study of an augmented museum experience.* HPL-2001–178 Technical Report # 20010726. Available: http://www.hpl.hp .com/techreports/2001/HPL-2001–178.html

Spitulnik, M. W. (2003). *Design principles for ubiquitous computing in education.* Center for Innovative Learning Technologies. University of California, Berkeley. Available: http://www.cilt.org/events/2003/UbiqDPAERA3.ppt

Staudt, C. (1999). Probing untested ground: Young students learn to use handheld computers. *The Concord Consortium.* [Online]. Available: http://www.concord.org/ pubs/1999fall/untested-ground.html

Staudt, C., & Hsi, S. (1999). Synergy projects and pocket computers. *@Concord 3*(3). Available: http://www.concord.org/library/1999spring/synergyproj.html

Tapscott, D. (1990). *Growing up digital.* New York: Hill Unlimited.

Technology foundation standards for all students. (2002). *International Society for Technology in Education.* [Online]. Available: http://cnets.iste.org/index2.html

Tenner, E. (1996). *Why things bite back: Technology and the revenge of unintended consequences.* New York: Alfred A. Knopf.

Thornburg, D. (2001). Campfires in cyberspace: Primordial metaphors for learning in the 21st century. *The Thornburg Center.* [Online]. Available: http://www.tcpd .org/thornburg/handouts/Campfires.pdf

Tinker, B., Staudt, C., & Walton, D. (2002). The handheld computer as field guide (Monday's lesson). *The Concord Consortium.* [Online]. Available: http://www .concord.org/newsletter/2002winter/monday_lesson.html

Tinker, R. (1996). The whole world in their hands. *The Concord Consortium.* [Online]. Available: http://www.ed.gov/Technology/Futures/tinker.html

Tinker, R. (1990). Teaching theory building. *The Concord Consortium.* [Online]. Available: http://www.concord.org/library/teachingtheory.html

Tinker, R. F., & Krajcik, J. S. (Eds.). (2001). *Portable technologies: Science learning in context.* New York: Kluwer Academic/Plenum Publishers.

Tristram, C. (2002, April). Hand-helds of tomorrow. *MIT's Magazine of Innovation Technology Review, 105*(3), 35–40.

Trotter, A. (2001, September 26). Handheld computing: New best tech tool or just a fad? *Education Week.*

12 learning interventions that combat technophobia. (2000, March). *Learning Circuits. ASTD.* [Online]. Available: http://www.learningcircuits.org/mar2000/mar2000_ elearn.html

Webb, W. (2001, July/August). PDA primer. *Online Learning.*

Wireless computer networking: WANs and LANs. [Online]. Available: http://www .tcet.unt.edu/wlan.htm

Woodruff, A., Aoki, P. M., Hurst, A., & Szymanski, M. H. (2001). *Electronic guidebooks and visitor attention.* To appear in proceedings of the International Cultural Heritage Informatics Meeting 2001.

Woodruff, A., Szymanski, M. H., Aoki, P. M., & Hurst, A. (2001). *The conversational role of electronic guidebooks.* To appear in proceedings of UBICOMP.

Zern, K. (2002). *Evaluation report—Handheld computers and learning in the informal museum setting.* Physical Science Exhibit Interpretation (PSEI). Boston: Museum of Science. Available: http://usight.concord.org/documents/probe_report.pdf

Credits

Beret Study Buddy: Vocab. application screen shots reprinted with permission of Beret Applications, LLC.

Screen shots of Sketchy, PicoMap, and iKWL reprinted with permission of the author, Elliot Soloway.

Screen shots of MathCars application reprinted with permission of the author, Jeremy Roschelle.

MicroJournal application software screen shots reprinted with permission of the author, LingleTech.com.

Palm English-English dictionary application reprinted with permission of Paragon Software (SHDD) www.penreader.com.

Screen shots of Platetarium application reprinted with permission of the author, Andreas Hofer.

Screen shots of Project@Hand software reprinted with permission of Natara Software.

Screen shots of QuickOffice application reprinted with permission of Quick Office, iGo Mobility Electronics Inc., Plano, Texas.

Screen shots of BFL application reprinted with permission of the author, bodyadvance.com and body-pro.com.

Screen shots of ImagiProbc and ImagiMath applications reprinted with permission of Imagiworks, Inc., Grass Valley, CA.

Screen shots of MobiMate application reprinted with permission of the author, MobiMate, Ltd, MobiMate.com.

Screen shots of TeamFlier reprinted with permission of author Ron Doerfler, TeamFlier software, EddieSoft.

Index

Activities for handheld computers. *See* Around the World in Eight Days Project; Chemical Periodicity Project; Concept Journaling Project; Continuous Water Cycle Project; Daily Log Project; Displaying Student Models Project; Field Guide Project; Fitness for Life Project; Frequent Sines Project; Impacting the World's Resources Project; Lost Tribes of Amazon Project; Pickle Pond Study; Rate of Change Project; Spelling Bee; Starry Sky Project; Surveying Homework Practices Project; Team Checklist Project; Viking Times Project

**CORWIN
PRESS**

The Corwin Press logo—a raven striding across an open book—represents the union of courage and learning. Corwin Press is committed to improving education for all learners by publishing books and other professional development resources for those serving the field of K–12 education. By providing practical, hands-on materials, Corwin Press continues to carry out the promise of its motto: **"Helping Educators Do Their Work Better."**